Your Other Family Doctor: A Veterinary Medical Memoir

Lorelei K. Hickman

Published by Lorelei Hickman, 2024.

While every precaution has been taken in the preparation of this book, the publisher assumes no responsibility for errors or omissions, or for damages resulting from the use of the information contained herein.

YOUR OTHER FAMILY DOCTOR: A VETERINARY MEDICAL MEMOIR

First edition. August 8, 2024.

Written by Lorelei K. Hickman.

Table of Contents

YOUR OTHER FAMILY DOCTOR
A Veterinary Medical Memoir
By Lorelei K. Hickman

CHAPTER ONE

If you're reading this, chances are you're an animal lover, and perhaps a caregiver to a companion animal. You are (or have been) a consumer of veterinary services. Maybe you're someone who works in the field of veterinary medicine- a DVM, a nurse or technician, a receptionist, a kennel attendant, a shelter volunteer. This book is for everyone with an interest in the way veterinary medicine is practiced in the United States. It will shock and sadden some people. It will anger others and make them extremely defensive. What I hope it will do is spark conversation and CHANGE. I hope that by sharing my own story as someone who has worked in the field- the experiences I've had, the things I've seen and heard- I can motivate companion animal caregivers in the U.S. to stand up and become proactive advocates for their animals every time they must see the vet, and to demand changes in the veterinary industry as a whole.

Veterinarians reading this will likely say that my experiences are anomalies which do not reflect the true state of veterinary medicine as it's been practiced in the past few decades. To that, all I can say is that I hope they're right; that perhaps I just had seven years of bad luck as I worked in several different veterinary hospitals in two different states. Maybe it was all coincidence when I saw the same problems playing out in every workplace- and suffered the effects of the same problems at every clinic where I was a client rather than an employee. Maybe it's another "anomaly" when I see other veterinary professionals on social media bemoaning the same issues. Maybe. Or just maybe, veterinary medicine needs a checkup on its HEART- now more than ever.

A conversation I encountered on social media recently between a pet caregiver and two veterinarians is disturbingly telling: The pet caregiver had been having a great deal of trouble trying to get a phone call back from her veterinarian to advise her on end-of-life issues for a terminally ill pet. She commented that when a veterinary practice cannot support a client through the most difficult part of pet guardianship because their schedule is too overbooked and the doctor cannot keep up with phone calls, the practice is "broken".

Two DVMs immediately responded with angry, defensive comments. One stated "their practice is not broken if they're busy and making enough to live on. You're just mad that they don't need to serve you to make a decent living." Another blamed her staff shortage on her clients for not purchasing pet insurance, and stated that "it's not about profit directly, but if people could afford veterinary care, more professionals would join the industry and stay."

Many have not stayed in the past few years. If an industry's lifeblood is its personnel, veterinary medicine has been bleeding out. But why? In the 2022 AVMA Census Of Veterinarians, "difficult or ungrateful clients" was the fourth most commonly cited reason for respondents wanting to leave the veterinary profession, with an equal number pointing to their clients as there were citing "challenging work/life balance".1 May of 2023 brought headlines about a shooting at a veterinary hospital in Kentucky in which an employee was killed by an irate client, reportedly in a dispute over the client's bill. This is the direction in which I fear the working relationship between DVMs and clients in the U.S. may be heading: a mutually mistrustful disharmony in which vets suspect every client of trying to get something for free, and clients feel unsupported, ignored, and ripped off. And the tragedy of the shooting notwithstanding- it's our companion animals who will suffer from this situation the most.

While the Covid-19 pandemic inarguably changed society and affected the economy in ways we are still struggling to understand and cope with, I see far too much blame being placed on the pandemic for the problems of inadequate staffing and inefficient management in the veterinary industry, which in my experience have *always* existed. I would go as far as to say that the pandemic is being used as a convenient excuse to sweep longstanding and ubiquitous problems under the rug and claim that these are new issues the industry is facing. They are NOT new. I cannot view them as new when I spent my career literally begging all my employers to *please* hire more staff (or to hire more astutely*)* so that we could keep up with the caseload and have adequate time to devote to every patient. Yes, pet adoptions and demand for services rose during the pandemic, and yes, a large number of veterinarians and vet techs burned out and left the profession at the same time, creating a "perfect storm" of too many pets for the number of veterinary staff who chose to remain- but again, this only exacerbated problems that were already pervasive in the industry. Covid brought all of veterinary medicine's chickens home to roost.

Liz Hughston, a vet tech and president of the National Veterinary Professionals Union, identified the problem precisely and succinctly when she told *The Atlantic* in 2022 that "the true depths of the staffing crisis hasn't been felt up until this point because, I think, we had what a lot of people thought was an inexhaustible supply of young starry-eyed people who want to work with puppies and kittens all day."[2] The profession has been plagued by higher than average turnover rates for decades, for various reasons that never had anything to do with Covid. If anything, the pandemic's fallout should serve as a wakeup call- to the veterinary industry as well as the entire world- that we *cannot* just keep doing things the way we've always done them.

Compared to the other professions that require an advanced degree- such as MDs, lawyers, dentists, etc.- the veterinary profession seems to have enjoyed a somewhat greater reputation among members of the public for remaining "good" and "noble". By and large, veterinarians are seen as caring, compassionate people, and are counted among "the good guys". In the 1999 film *Fight Club* (based on the novel of the same name by Chuck Palahniuk), the character of Tyler Durden is an anarchist who wants to tear down all of society- yet, even *he* evidently believes so earnestly in the goodness of the veterinary profession that he takes it upon himself to strongly motivate a pre-vet student who is considering dropping out, and emphasizes that "animals and stuff" are worth caring for. As a society, our tendency seems to be to view every veterinarian as a combination of Dr. Doolittle and James Herriot; kindly souls who do what they do as a pure labor of love, and who should always be given the benefit of the doubt when that image is in danger of tarnishing.

But veterinarians are not "better" humans- on average- than anyone else, and veterinary medicine didn't begin with the most humane and noble of aspirations. It didn't begin with the express goals of improving animal welfare or relieving animal suffering, despite the prominence of these things in the Veterinary Oath sworn by all new licensees since the middle of the last century. It began in ancient times (various

sources trace its origins back thousands of years BCE,
finding evidence in ancient civilizations such as Egypt,
China, Mesopotamia, India and Greece) as a way to utilize
animals more effectively, safely, and efficiently. Sick livestock
didn't produce good meat and could make humans sick as
well, and sick or injured "beasts of burden" couldn't pull
plows or chariots, so something had to be done. In fact, the
Latin terms *veheri* ("to pull") and *veterinarius*- from which
came the terms "veterinarian" and "veterinary"- meant
"pertaining to beasts of burden". 3,4 For most of the
profession's history, simply maintaining and protecting
animal-derived resources was the primary focus, despite the
fact that humans also began keeping animals as companions
with no utilitarian function in these ancient civilizations as
well. (One possible exception to this exploitative attitude
was in ancient Egypt,5 where animals enjoyed an elevated
status compared to other societies of the time, valued for
their religious significance as well as for food or for the tasks
they could perform.)

The rise of Christianity as a dominant cultural force resulted
in the complete suppression of veterinary science for
centuries, since the Church decreed that animals were not
worthy of medical treatment (and also discouraged scientific
research of all types). Thus, it wasn't until the 1700s brought
the Age of Enlightenment that veterinary medicine's
"rebirth" could take place.6

The first veterinary school to be founded after the Church's
destruction of most of the ancient civilizations' literature
on the subject was in France in 1762. This was deemed
necessary to curb the deaths of cattle from bubonic plague,

but again- this was for the benefit of humans, not the cattle themselves. Even in modern times, a large part of the role of veterinarians in our society has been to maintain the health of farm animals and inspect facilities to ensure food safety and contain the spread of zoonotic diseases which can be transmitted from animals to humans. (These are two areas which have presented greater and greater challenges as animal agriculture becomes more industrialized and more focused on mass production.) They have also conducted medical, surgical, and pharmaceutical research using lab animals, and treated other, more modern kinds of "working animals" such as dogs being used by the military and police to perform dangerous or specialized tasks. As late as the 1980s, 40% of new veterinary school graduates in the United States were still specializing in treatment of livestock animals or other areas of practice relating to food production, whereas today only about 3-4% are.[7] (This in itself is cause for concern in an era when we must be on guard against the next pandemic which could originate from poor livestock husbandry, but that is not the focus of this writing.)

What changed in the last 40 years? Petkeeping in the U.S. has been steadily on the rise since the 1980s, and so has the amount of money that pet caretakers spend at the vet clinic. Thus, more and more vet school graduates have been choosing to go into companion animal practice. More and more, Americans have come to view their pets as family members, and veterinarians have encouraged us to view them as "your other family doctor". While that may give us a warm-fuzzy feeling, in many ways it's little more than a marketing catchphrase. Animals obviously do not enjoy

the same legal or social status in the US as humans do, and
for all its attempts to imitate and follow in the footsteps of
human medicine, endeavoring to provide the same degree
of technologically advanced diagnostics and surgical
techniques, veterinary medicine is fundamentally different,
and is practiced in fundamentally different ways from
human medicine.

Chief among these differences-and of special concern to pet
caregivers- is the fact that veterinary medicine is largely
unregulated in comparison, with doctors and practitioners
subject to far less scrutiny and far fewer disciplinary
measures than their counterparts in human medicine. To
put it bluntly, bad vets get away with a lot more than bad
MDs do, and they always have. Pet caregivers have little
recourse if their beloved companion is harmed through a
veterinarian's negligence or incompetence- they may sue for
malpractice, but historically these cases have been difficult
for caregivers to prove, and they yield comparatively little
compensation due to the legal status of animals as mere
property. In most cases, a caregiver can only hope to recoup
the money spent on the pet's care in addition to the "market
or replacement value" of the animal.[8] This utterly disrespects
the human-animal bond and the depth of emotion that
people can feel for a family member of a different species.

Furthermore, the job requirements for veterinary support
staff members such as nurses/technicians are far less rigorous
than the requirements for nurses in human medicine,
despite the fact that veterinary nurses often *also* effectively
end up functioning as radiographers, pharmacists,
anesthesiologist assistants, phlebotomists, laboratory
technologists, and customer service representatives in

addition to being the personnel who are the most directly involved in patient monitoring and care. *One* staff member at your local vet clinic will usually be doing the jobs of *multiple* people at the human medical hospital down the street, but in many states, there are no pre-hiring requirements for them to meet whatsoever; a veterinary practice can hire anyone for the position- even if they have no prior veterinary experience- and train them on the job rather than having to pay a higher wage to a candidate who has completed a veterinary nursing training program and been licensed. They are still legally able to call these people veterinary technicians or nurses- despite this amounting to false advertising- and pet caregivers are none the wiser. 9 (An organization called the Veterinary Nurse Initiative (veterinarynurse.org) is working to help establish and promote standardized educational requirements and credentials for veterinary support staff performing the tasks of technicians and nurses, as well as legal title protection with penalties for its misuse.)

It's this lack of regulation or effective oversight that undoubtedly resulted in many of the troubling things I saw going on in my workplaces. I was one of a countless number of these uncredentialed veterinary technician/nurses; one of those "starry-eyed young people" who entered the field thinking I'd landed my dream job- because I *had*. Let me make one thing very clear before going any further: I did not set out to write this memoir because I hate veterinarians or the veterinary profession, despite a lot of negative experiences. On the contrary- I *love* the profession, which is why I am critical of its shortcomings and want to see it address its problems and do better. I gave my all to my work, and it broke my heart again and again. The current state of veterinary medicine- as more and more independent hospitals are being swallowed up by corporate chains- is *shattering* it.

CHAPTER TWO

"Being admitted to the profession of veterinary medicine, I solemnly swear to use my scientific knowledge and skills for the benefit of society through the protection of animal health and welfare, the prevention and relief of animal suffering, the conservation of animal resources, the promotion of public health, and the advancement of medical knowledge. I will practice my profession conscientiously, with dignity, and in keeping with the principles of veterinary medical ethics. I accept as a lifelong obligation the continual improvement of my professional knowledge and competence."[10,11]

As a child, whenever I was asked what I wanted to be when I grew up, my answer was always "a vet"- from the moment I first learned what vets are and what they do. I didn't learn until many years later that there was actually a Veterinarian's Oath similar to the Hippocratic Oath for medical doctors, but the notion of "preventing and relieving animal suffering" nevertheless struck me as being central and intrinsic to their job, and to my mind, no higher calling existed or could be imagined.

Like many children, I was fascinated by animals of all kinds, and growing up without siblings in an isolated, rural area left me on my own for the most part, except for our family's pets. From a very young age I thought of animals unquestionably as family members as well as my closest friends. I was encouraged in this thinking by my parents, who would refer to our dogs as "your brother and sister" (despite never allowing them on the furniture, in an odd but common bit of cognitive dissonance). When it was time for their annual vet visit, my parents took me along, and I watched everything avidly and told myself that this would be my world one day. When one of them was hit by a car and needed emergency treatment, it was really hammered home to me that veterinarians are the difference between life and death *just like* "people doctors" are (and my parents started keeping both dogs indoors and walking them on leashes after that!).

Of course, it didn't take me long to realize that veterinarians also have to put animals "to sleep", and this was the first thing to give me pause when contemplating my future career. Would I be able to do that? My mind shied away from it whenever I tried to answer.

By the time I reached high school, my mind had also begun to shy away from the higher mathematics which I knew would be inescapable in any science-based career, and to gravitate instead toward language and the humanities, so I gradually let go of my childhood dream and began to think instead about writing. I majored in English when I went to college- not because it was necessarily my passion, but because it was what I was naturally good at with minimal effort required. My plan was to earn my paycheck through journalism while moonlighting as a novelist, but unfortunately, I came up with this plan at approximately the same moment that the newborn Internet changed the world of print journalism forever, making it seem like a much less promising or stable career.

In 1997 I was twenty-five years old and stuck in one of many dead-end jobs-selling and tearing tickets at a movie theater- when I decided to take a "correspondence course" to train to be a veterinary assistant. The very term "correspondence course" seems quaint and outdated now; the idea of receiving academic course materials *in the old-fashioned postal mail* and having to send them back the same way after completion seems like the mythology of an ancient culture. And little did I know at the time how very unnecessary my efforts were; taking that course made no difference whatsoever to my future job prospects within the veterinary field, as it turned out. That's not to say that the course was entirely worthless; on the contrary, I did feel that I learned a good deal. It just wasn't *required* for me to know anything when I was hired for my first veterinary position. Taking the course showed that I had passion and initiative, but as for what I knew? - my prospective employers couldn't have cared less. In fact- I would come to know all too well- the less people knew when they started, the better the clinic owners liked it.

My veterinary career officially began in May of 1998 when I was hired for a receptionist position (back when we were still *called* receptionists and not the much-more-important-sounding "customer service representatives" of today) at a small companion-animal hospital serving the neighborhood of Inman Park in Atlanta, Georgia. This hospital was unique in several ways; it was owned and operated by two lesbians in a predominantly LGBT neighborhood, for starters. It was an extremely diverse and progressive workplace and ahead of its time in that regard.

The business manager- a no-nonsense woman I'll call "Roberta"- and the head DVM- who I'll call "Dr. F."- were former romantic partners who seemed to have successfully put their shared past aside to focus on running what was primarily a low-cost spay/neuter clinic for cats and dogs, although they saw other medical cases as well. Dr. F. had already had a full career as a psychologist and had walked away from that profession and put herself through veterinary school with the express goal of spaying and neutering as many cats and dogs as she could, in response to what she saw as the most pressing issue in veterinary medicine. She even required all her clients to "fix" their animals by one year of age if they wanted to remain clients at her hospital; if they didn't, she would politely copy their pets' records for them and refer them somewhere else. Roberta came from the hospitality industry, a veteran of hotel front desks. Together they'd built a veterinary practice that had- over the decade of its existence- earned the fierce loyalty of the surrounding community, and only partially because the community wanted to support "our own".

Most of that didn't matter to me when I started working for them, however. I was just happy to be working at a veterinary clinic- *any* veterinary clinic, truth be told. It was an amazing feeling to wake up and get ready for work each day believing that what I did that day would *matter.* I'd never experienced that before. I was accustomed to thinking about my job in terms of how many hours I would be forced to be there in order to pay for groceries that week and make rent at the end of the month; how much time it would take away from my life and my *real* work (which I still believed was writing the Great American Novel). What I would actually *do* during all those hours was of far less consequence to me; it didn't really bear thinking about at all. But now there would be no more wasting endless hours and days of my life on tasks that were utterly meaningless to me, and worse- they were meaningless to the world, as well. Before, no one in their right mind would ever have had a reason to care whether I was good at my job or not, or whether I was even there at all. But now it could literally mean the difference between life and death for a cat or a dog. *I* could *be* that difference.

That knowledge gave extra weight to everything I did, even if it was "just" filing. Making sure that medical record got filed correctly meant it would be found quicker the next time it was needed, and that would save valuable minutes that could mean a better outcome for an animal in crisis. For the first time in my life, I actually felt proud to put on my work uniform, with its hospital logo embroidered right over my heart. For the first time, I actually felt like I was part of a *team* united for a common goal- namely, providing the best veterinary care available in the Atlanta metro area.

I soon found myself beginning to wish that everyone I worked with felt the same way, however. I wished everyone on the team had the same attention to detail and the same determination to get everything right the first time. I wished everyone could leave their personal problems and drama at the door when they arrived at work and focus on the patients, who were the reason we were all there. At the time, I believed our team had more than the average amount of workplace drama due to Roberta's habit of hiring people from the LGBT community who "needed a second chance in life" (meaning they'd been fired from other jobs), but in hindsight, I doubt it made that much difference. I didn't yet know how rampant a problem employee turnover is within the veterinary industry; I thought it was something that plagued *us* in particular.

Usually, people would end up quitting on their own; after coming to the rescue of someone who'd desperately needed a second chance, Roberta was usually loath to turn around and fire them *again*. Sometimes, though, this would mean that we kept an employee much longer than we should have, and sometimes it would impact the patients.

I remember one incident where a boarding dog- the last one to be let out in the exercise yard behind the hospital near the end of the day- was forgotten out there when the hospital was shut down and everyone went home. It was a chilly night, and the dog was left without access to food, water, bedding, or shelter until the staff returned the next morning, and we were lucky he hadn't managed to dig underneath the fence and escape. Also luckily, the dog was no worse for wear after his night under the stars, but this was clearly beside the point; what had happened was unacceptable. At least *that* time, the person responsible for leaving the dog outside all night did get fired.

It didn't take very long for me to become the longest-lasting receptionist on the team- a "senior" member responsible for training each new receptionist in turn. I then got a crash course in all the ways employee turnover slows down a business, decimating its productivity and efficacy as the seasoned members of the team must stop what they're doing in order to teach the new people *everything*. And we really did have to teach them everything, because Dr. F. was quite insistent that she did not *want* anyone who'd worked at a veterinary hospital before. She had a very particular way of doing things, I was told, and she said that people who'd worked at other animal hospitals would just have to "unlearn" everything they knew in order to work for her.

Looking back on it now, I would characterize Dr. F.'s "particular way of doing things" as simply being motivated by *purpose* rather than profit. As I've said, veterinary medicine was her second career- seemingly more of an avocation, really- to keep herself busy into her retirement years. The main goal of her practice was to provide low-cost spay/neuter services to the community and to educate caregivers about the importance and the benefits of spaying and neutering their animals. She was on a *mission*. She was not interested in seeing as many patients as she could possibly see in a day. She was not interested in generating as much revenue as she could possibly generate in a day.

In fact, she would strictly limit the number of cases that could be dropped off each day, and once we reached that limit, the receptionists were to refer clients to other hospitals in the area unless they had a legitimate emergency. (When in doubt, we could ask Dr. F., but we always risked a tongue-lashing if we interrupted her without excellent reason. On one memorable occasion, the entire reception area of the hospital- clients included- got to hear Dr. F. yelling that blood in the stool was not a true emergency and "I don't go to the doctor every time I have blood in *my* stool!")

Thus, a sizable portion of my job was getting medical history from the client to help determine whether their animal should be seen by a doctor, and how urgent it was. I had to know what constituted a danger sign and what didn't; what kinds of things were normal and what was not; what had the potential to become a bigger problem and what was probably safe for the client to monitor for improvement at home. This kind of knowledge is being outsourced nowadays, as companies like Mascotte Health (which calls itself a "veterinary practice operator") emerge to offer veterinary clinics "tech-enabled support infrastructure solutions such as virtual triage" and to "strategically pair" licensed veterinary professionals with their partner clinics. [12]

This strikes me as a needlessly complicated way of saying that the next time you call your vet clinic, chances are the person answering the phone won't even be an actual employee of that clinic and will not know you or your pet. (And for the money the clinic must undoubtedly spend for these "tech-enabled support infrastructure solutions", they could likely hire and pay a licensed veterinary professional of their very own!) In my own experience from the client's perspective in the years since I left the profession, this kind of triage-by-phone had gone almost nonexistent before Covid made it necessary everywhere; the favored practice at most hospitals seemed to be doing the opposite and simply telling every client to bring the pet in if they were concerned about something. That not only saved staff time on every phone call, but more importantly, it generated more revenue for the clinic. (I suspect this was the kind of thing Dr. F.'s employees had to "unlearn" if they had come from other vet hospitals.)

There are lots of rationalizations for this "never say no" attitude- "we want to help as many pets as we can" is usually chief among them, but once your hospital has taken in more cases than the staff can keep up with and they make preventable errors as a result, you're no longer helping; you've become part of the problem. Dr. F. understood that, and she made sure the rest of us understood it as well.

Preventable errors in human medicine are acknowledged to be a serious and rampant issue, with numerous government agencies, patients' rights organizations, and university think tanks all focused on how to reduce their frequency (and with many people involved in these groups saying that it's still not enough!), but I am unaware of any truly comparable effort to tackle the same problem in the veterinary world. It's a fact of life that human beings make mistakes, and it's another fact of life that they will make *more* mistakes when they're exhausted and juggling too many tasks at once. Veterinary hospitals do not have the same legal obligation as human hospitals to provide care for every patient arriving on the premises, so they also do not have that as an excuse for biting off more than their staff can chew, day after day. While I suspect that Dr. F.'s policy of limiting cases had as much to do with her own work/life balance as anything else, it nevertheless communicated to her clients that she was serious about devoting her entire attention to each pet when they did need to be seen, and I believe it was part of why her client base was so loyal.

It was far from her only idiosyncrasy, however, and Dr. F. was not easy to work for. I could see that objectively, but again- because I had no real frame of reference yet, I thought it was part of why *this* hospital had so much turnover. Even the doctors changed frequently. At one point Dr. F. was the only DVM we had.

It never occurred to me at the time that some of these other doctors- all of them fresh out of school so that Dr. F. could mold them in her own image- could have had issues with the way Dr. F. practiced medicine rather than just experiencing a clash of personalities. Much of what went on "in the back" was a mystery to me; Dr. F. didn't allow other personnel in the treatment area as a general rule- only the DVMs and techs. Anyone else "would just get in the way". I believed Roberta's assertion that Dr. F. was the best veterinarian she knew, and most of our clients echoed it. It wasn't until I was finally successful in persuading Roberta to let me move away from the reception desk and start training as a tech myself that I started seeing things that made me question it.

Roberta was reluctant at first to let me make the move. By that time I'd been promoted to become the front desk supervisor, making the employee work schedules for the other receptionists and handling inventory management and ordering in addition to my other duties. I was very much still needed at the front desk, and she thought we had enough techs. (We did *not* have enough- at least, not according to any of the techs!) But I was persistent, because I wanted to learn more and be more hands-on with the patients, doing the actual *caring* for them. I wanted to be cross-trained "in the back" as well as on the front line facing the public, so that I could better understand the actual work involved in the different kinds of cases we saw and could better explain things to clients, as well.

Roberta still expressed doubts, telling me that she didn't think I had the right personality for the hands-on work. "You don't seem like someone who likes getting dirty," I remember her saying. I laughed that off, thinking she meant I was too "girly", but there was probably some truth in her perception. Years later I would conclude that I really *didn't* have the right personality to be a vet tech, although it had nothing to do with being afraid to get dirty. I had a tendency to become too emotionally attached to patients- especially the cats- because I really took to heart the popular industry axiom "we treat your pet like they're our own". I genuinely cared about *every* patient just as much as I cared about my own "fur babies" waiting for me at home, and that was probably a recipe for burnout at warp speed; there are very good reasons that medical professionals in the human sphere are discouraged or prohibited from treating their own family members, after all. (No such caveat exists in veterinary medicine as far as I am aware, although it certainly should!)

But that was far in the future when Roberta finally relented and said that I could train as a tech for part of each week if I also continued working at the front desk and handling the supervisor duties. I was elated. Soon I was learning how to identify various intestinal parasites in fecal samples under a microscope, how to run heartworm tests for dogs and FIV/ Leukemia tests for cats, and how to operate an autoclave and make up surgical instrument packs. I also learned restraint techniques to hold animals still for physical exams and venipuncture, and even how to draw the blood myself (I practiced alone at home on the prominent veins on the backs of my own hands, to be certain that I wasn't going to hurt the patients!). I learned the basics of taking X rays, of monitoring anesthesia during surgery, and even how to do an entire "simple" surgery myself, at least in theory: neutering male cats.

This was the quickest, least invasive routine procedure we did at our clinic, even more so than neutering male dogs. (Feline neuters could be done SO quickly, in fact, Dr. F. didn't even bother intubating the patients, which I later learned is below the standard of care for *any* general anesthetic procedure). I was nonplussed to learn that Dr. F. permitted her (unlicensed!) technicians to perform this particular surgery themselves. She delegated it like any other "minor" duties when she had more complicated cases she was dealing with, and somehow this was viewed as normal by Roberta and everyone else there (although perhaps *not* with the newly graduated associate doctors going in and out of our revolving front door!)

While an oft-repeated bit of advice to overwhelmed DVMs today *is* to delegate more tasks to nurses and technicians, this can *never* extend to performing surgery. This is illegal in every state, regardless of how the state defines the terms "veterinary technician" or "veterinary nurse" and regardless of whether they are in fact legally licensed as nurses (which Dr. F.'s staff was *not*.) I flatly refused to do it. I may not have immediately realized that deliberately skipping intubation during anesthesia was as bad a practice as it is, but I wasn't naïve enough to believe it was OK to let people operate on cats when they'd been working for a *catering* business the previous month. This was my first inkling that the way Dr. F. did things might not always be exactly the *right* way.

It's mind-boggling to me now- looking back- that she was so nonchalant about it, despite the terror she had of being sued. Every conversation with every client had to be meticulously documented in their pet's medical record in the event she might face a malpractice suit, but she could blithely throw laws *and* common sense out the window in this way seemingly without giving it a second thought. It's very telling that a DVM with a phobia of being sued STILL thought she could run her clinic basically any way she wanted to...and be *correct* about that. As long as no client heard it or saw it, she seemed to believe it would be fine. Certainly no one else was going to be watching her or checking up on her. (I suspect that her inordinate fear of a malpractice suit came primarily from her previous career as a psychologist and *not* from any experience she had as a veterinarian or any training she received in vet school. The threat of being sued for malpractice-even still today- is essentially a monster without teeth, since veterinary malpractice suits are almost criminally limited in their scope and in what grieving pet caregivers can hope to recoup. As a result, it's often seemed to me that many DVMs worry much more about the cost of their malpractice insurance than they do about ever being found *guilty* of malpractice.)

There were other things that began to disturb me, as well. I assisted Dr. F. with surgeries enough times to know that she would often *recycle suture material* that had already been used on a patient. If there was a significant amount of suture material left over from the packet after a surgery, she would simply dunk it in a jar of Nolvasan (chlorhexidine) disinfectant-needle and all- and re-use it later for stitching up external wounds on outpatient cases. This made me cringe. She also recycled single-use disposable syringes after autoclaving them, as well- something that the packaging on the syringes expressly forbade doing. She didn't believe in giving animals pain medication after most spay/neuter surgeries, saying it would prevent them from limiting their own activity during the recovery period (this was a common belief in veterinary medicine until fairly recently and was a widespread practice among older practitioners. Conveniently for them, however, foregoing pain medication *also* helped them keep the clinic's costs of doing surgery lower, which was probably at least an equal concern for most of them.)

It was very hard for me to reconcile this new information about my employer with the previous picture I'd had of her. It seemed she was not as far beyond reproach as I'd been led to believe, and I suppose I started making noises to that effect. At the time, however, I was trying to stay focused on the bigger picture, and the bigger picture that I could perceive indicated that-all things considered- Dr. F.'s vision still seemed better to me overall than most of the alternatives.

As a front-desk supervisor with a focus on keeping very detailed medical records, it was my observation that the records kept by the vast majority of our local competitor clinics were woefully inadequate in comparison. (In particular, I learned that the records kept by "PetSmart vets"- later to be known as the corporate entity of Banfield- were considered by *all* of the doctors I worked with to be the absolute worst of the worst, with the PetSmart doctors essentially never bothering to write any notes at *all*!)

Dr. F. taught us that the medical record was the foundation upon which the entire practice rested and depended, and each patient's individual file was essentially "a Bible" instructing veterinary professionals in how to treat that individual patient. We were *never* to approach her with a question or a message about a pet unless we had that pet's record in our hands to give to her. Based on the slipshod recordkeeping I was seeing myself (some of them didn't even have the patient's age or sex recorded!), I could well understand how other hospitals could commit major errors like admitting the wrong patient for surgery or neglecting to give a vital medication while the pet was boarding. We would sometimes hear horror stories like this from clients with friends or relatives that used other vet clinics.

So Dr. F. wasn't perfect, I conceded to myself, but I could still believe her heart was in the right place. Financial considerations played a huge part; it was presented to me again and again by Roberta that Dr. F. did many of the things she did *in the way that she did them* as part of an effort to be fiscally conservative and keep operating costs down for the clinic, thereby keeping fees down for the clients. Again, I believe this is part of why her client base was so loyal, but this is also one of the dangers of "old school" practitioners such as TV's popular "Dr. Pol" (who has been filmed performing surgery on patients without benefit of even such basics as sterile gloves). Their clients may love them for keeping their fees down, but their *patients* may end up paying back some of the cost in actual quality of care. Cheap medicine which subjects patients to unnecessary risks is never really a bargain, and this is how I learned that "good business" and "good medicine" are essentially incompatible. But in a capitalist society which has completely embraced the concept of for-profit healthcare for humans as well as our companion animals, business becomes the priority far too often.

Does every clinic with reasonable fees subject its patients to risk of infections (or worse) by cutting corners? No- that isn't what I'm saying (and to be fair, if any of Dr. F.'s patients ever did have problems related to her way of practicing, I was unaware of it). Nor do clinics with exorbitant fees guarantee a higher margin of safety for patients undergoing procedures there. The quality of a clinic's care or a doctor's heart can't be determined by fees alone, but if those fees are markedly lower than those of other clinics in the area, I want pet caregivers to at least be curious enough to ask questions about *why and how,* rather than simply celebrating it. Be sure the why and how are acceptable to you.

CHAPTER THREE

The new millennium came and went. "Y2K"- for all the anxiety it caused- ended up being no big deal. The only thing that seemed different about society was a new unspoken cynicism- another "end of the world" had been averted and proved to be smoke and mirrors, leading many people to believe that the world as we knew it would *never* end, come what may.

Things were changing at my workplace, however. Three years after I signed on, Roberta and Dr. F. made the decision to sell the clinic and move on to the next chapter in their lives. The buyer turned out to be someone quite illustrious- or at least, "illustrious-adjacent": a relative of Jim Fowler, co-host of the TV show "Mutual of Omaha's Wild Kingdom". (I will here call this DVM "Dr. G.", since there is already a "Dr. F." in my story.) The buzz around the water cooler was that "Dr. G." treated all manner of exotic animals- not just cats and dogs- and most of us on the staff were initially excited about the prospect of getting to work with and learn about a veritable zoo menagerie. (As it turned out, we would still see mostly just dogs and cats, but there was the occasional exotic case that spiced things up. One of the most memorable was an egg-bound iguana who required "mouth-to-mouth" resuscitation through a drinking straw.)

Dr. G. was already the owner of a mobile veterinary practice with advanced capabilities extending to surgery and diagnostics- which at that time was almost unheard of and is still fairly rare today. But he felt limited in his potential for expansion that way and was keen to acquire a

brick-and-mortar clinic to attract more clients, in addition
to inheriting an already well-established clientele. He was
out to grow his practice and make money, and he didn't
make a big secret of that fact. It was my first introduction
to growth and profit as acknowledged goals in veterinary
medicine.

Massive changes quickly started sweeping through our little
hospital, and none of them were good. Dr. F.'s policy of
limiting the caseload so that every patient could receive
adequate time and attention was the first thing on the
chopping block. Now, scheduling was a free-for-all, with
the receptionists instructed to encourage *every* client with
a concern- large or small!!- to bring the pet in *that day* if
possible. (Before long I was wondering why we bothered to
make appointments at all, since we would *never* adhere to
the schedule anymore.) The waiting area degenerated into
constant chaos as appointments backed up and wait times
extended longer and longer. Clients began to grumble, and
the receptionists had to make excuses and apologize for our
"growing pains" during this "transitional period".

But it wasn't a transitional period, and they weren't just
growing pains. It was The New Way, and the chaos was quite
by design. Dr. G. seemed to *thrive* on chaos; his motto was
"the busier, the better!" and I'm sure this is a sentiment
shared- back then as well as today- by 99.999% of
veterinarians who own their own practices. But "busier" is
only "better" for the business owner's wallet- *nothing else.*
The busier the hospital, the more the quality of care, staff
morale and mental health, customer service, and even basic
cleanliness will all suffer, and I want pet caretakers to
remember this the next time they're stuck in an

overcrowded waiting room long past their appointment time. If the front office (that the clinic is willing to show the world) is chaotic, it's a fairly safe bet that it will be many times *more* chaotic "in the back" where your beloved pet will likely be taken for treatment... out of your sight. Chaos is a convenient scapegoat that can be blamed for all manner of errors, oversights, and failures. Chaos can be used to mask the symptoms of much deeper problems in a hospital.

Dr. G. might have thrived in chaos, but most of the rest of us did not, since it was considerably harder for the support staff to recognize or appreciate the dollar signs resulting from said chaos (our paychecks still didn't reflect them!). Most of us were still used to Dr. F.'s way of doing things and were having trouble adjusting and keeping up with the new pace. Some left and were replaced.

One technician- hired shortly before the clinic changed hands- had almost been dismissed by Roberta because she'd come to regret hiring her (which was saying something!), but under Dr. G.'s command she'd evidently been promoted instead (I say "evidently" because nothing was ever said about it officially.) I'll call her "Jessica". Jessica was the one person on the staff who seemed to welcome chaos in equal measure to Dr. G., and she seemed to have ingratiated herself to him and his wife "Shelly" (who'd taken over for Roberta as the business manager). Now she was angling to position herself as Dr. G's indispensable "girl Friday".

I didn't care for this development because I'd agreed with Roberta that Jessica had been a mistake to hire in the first place. She did not listen to instructions. She did not follow directions. She did not follow through on many tasks, often leaving things incomplete or failing to record treatments in patients' charts when they *were* completed. She did not seem to grasp the importance of things like accurately logging the amounts of controlled drugs that were used each day, or making sure a thermometer was disinfected between patients. She pretended to know a lot more about veterinary medicine than she actually did know (being just as unlicensed as the rest of us), and she would often talk down to her fellow support staff members. She even talked down to the newest DVM to join the team, criticizing her for a perceived "lack of confidence" in diagnosing patients and saying she needed to stop asking Dr. G. for his opinion all the time. (It is by no means abnormal for a new vet school graduate to be mentored by their employer in their first job; this is in fact a fairly standard practice and something that savvy new graduates look for when considering job offers.)13

Once more I was forced to re-evaluate the people I was working for and the environment I was working in, and this time it wasn't as easy to convince myself that I was still in the best place I could be. My workplace was becoming undeniably toxic, and unrecognizable as the same place I'd started out. Staff tensions multiplied exponentially under the weight of the new productivity mandates and the palpably weird and undefined role that Jessica now seemed to be playing. Dr. G. seemed perfectly willing to sit back and let her do anything she wanted, and I had a bad feeling about it.

There were two incidents that together served as a deciding factor for me, and they both occurred in the surgery room. The first came shortly after Dr. G. took ownership of the hospital and performed the first-ever declaw surgery to take place on the premises. The second came when one of my own cats developed a suspicious mass on his shoulder blade after getting a corticosteroid injection there, and Dr. G. almost killed him with an anesthetic overdose when we were going to remove the mass.

At the turn of the millennium, declawing cats was not considered to be anywhere near as controversial as it is today. (And *despite* the current controversy- and also despite a growing belief among the American public that "most vets have stopped doing it"- declawing does remain fully legal in 47 out of 50 states as of this writing, and is still performed by the majority of practicing veterinarians in the United States. The Paw Project-the leading organization aiming to end the practice and educate the public about its adverse effects- estimates that anywhere from 25-43% of all cats in American homes were still being declawed in 2023[14]).

If there is any *single* thing I could point to as a reliable measure of whether a veterinary clinic is a good one or not, it *absolutely* would be the question of whether they declaw cats. That's a far cry from my stance on the issue before I'd started working in veterinary medicine or had lived with any cats. I once assumed that if I had cats, I would *want* them declawed. I had no reason to believe there was anything wrong with it if it was a common procedure that nearly every veterinarian did... *right*?

It wasn't until I started working for Dr. F. that I was given any inkling that declawing might be harmful to cats. Her refusal to perform this barbaric alteration was one of the things that set her practice apart and made it truly unique for its time. I'd never known prior to working there that "declawing" is actually a misnomer and that the surgery goes far beyond "removing the claws" by amputating the entire last bone from each of the cat's toes, because the claws grow directly *from* that bone. This may sound bad enough, but to fully appreciate the degree to which this mutilation can negatively impact a cat's quality of life, one must understand that cats are *digitigrade* animals who bear their weight and walk on their toes as opposed to the flat part of their feet the way we humans walk (which is known as "plantigrade").

Removing a cat's toe tips and claws affects their ability to properly maintain their balance, run, climb, hunt, play, stretch, groom, and scent mark their territory using glands on their paws. It adversely affects their entire biomechanical functioning, causing them to shift their weight off their front paws and resulting in misalignment of the wrists, elbows, shoulders, and back. It predisposes the patient to arthritis and other painful disorders of the musculoskeletal system through abnormal wear and tear on the joints. It has been linked to bone cancer, obesity, and diabetes in some cats, and to emotional and behavioral problems such as biting and litterbox avoidance as cats attempt to cope with chronic pain and the loss of their first line of defense.

In his excellent 2018 book *The Theory Of Mammalian Life,* Canadian vet Jordyn Hewer, DVM states "this amputation causes pain, acute and chronic, and prevents the expression of natural behavior by restricting (cats') ability for movement. There is no valid medical or scientific reason to perform this procedure. It is completely medically unnecessary and for this reason, the Western world has predominantly banned it under the premise of animal cruelty. However, Canada and the United States are exceptions in that the procedure remains legal yet controversial as an elective procedure".15 As of the spring of 2024, nine of the ten Canadian provinces have joined the rest of the world in banning declawing, leaving the United States as the last major nation to hold out on doing so.

Today, the big corporate veterinary franchises such as Banfield, VCA, and Blue Pearl have made headlines for dropping declawing from their menu of services (and contributing to the *illusion* that "most vets" have stopped doing it), but in the late 1990s and early 2000s, anyone speaking out against declawing was generally considered to be a bit of a "crazy cat person" regardless of their gender.

This might be the time for me to insert a few words about cats in veterinary medicine in general. The biggest takeaway I want to impress upon any cat lover reading this is that *cats are treated as second-class citizens in the world of vet med in the United States. Cat caretakers must be STRONGER AND BETTER INFORMED advocates for their pets than dog lovers need to be.*

Why is this? Because veterinary medicine and our society in general are extremely "dog-centric". Veterinary medicine has prioritized dogs for decades because pet caretakers who spend money at veterinary clinics tend to spend *more* money on their dogs than their cats. (This probably goes back centuries to the days when dogs were viewed as essential for "work" functions, and they incurred more injuries as a result of those "jobs").

Also, dogs are much better than cats are at letting their caretakers know when they're hurting or feeling sick. As small animals targeted by larger predators in the wild, cats are biologically hardwired to hide signs of pain, illness, or weakness which would mark them as easy prey, and this stoicism tends to work against them when it comes to getting their health needs addressed.

As a result of the public's greater spending on their dogs, not only do vet school students overwhelmingly tend to focus on dogs and dogs' issues, but pharmaceutical companies often will only bother to go through enough rounds of testing for their products to be FDA approved for dogs, while completely ignoring cats. Many drugs used in veterinary settings have not been approved for use in cats, but are used "off label" according to the guidelines for dogs, so that the pharmaceutical company's profits on the drugs are larger. These are just some of the reasons why today you will hear some prominent and esteemed veterinarians such as Nicole Martell-Moran (DVM, MPH, DABVP) saying things like "cats were left in the dark a little bit, and were treated like small dogs"[16] when she was in school (not that this has changed that significantly since she graduated in 2009).

There was also- at least at the time I'm describing- a saying among many in the veterinary field that "cats are the redheaded stepchildren of veterinary medicine". I heard it said quite a few times. It's the kind of thing professionals will acknowledge among *themselves* but will *never* say to clients or others outside the profession. (For anyone unfamiliar with the phrase-which dates back at least to 1910 but the etymology of which is much debated- a "redheaded stepchild" is defined as "a person or thing that is unfairly disliked or maltreated"[17].)

I had already gathered- even before hearing this- that there are quite a few people working in vet med who don't really like cats or enjoy working with them. I was sensitive to it because of my own cat Merlin, who I'd adopted as a semi-feral kitten *from* the clinic not long after I'd started working there. Assumed orphaned at three weeks of age and brought in by a client of the clinic, he'd been a hissing, squirmy, swatting patient from day one. He'd tried to bite more than once, and he was very fortunate to have been brought to us rather than to the city animal shelter, where he would most likely have been euthanized as "unadoptable" while still a baby, just because he was terrified. He'd come a long way since then, but he would always have a reputation among the techs for being "fractious" (or "spicy", as it's often called today), and nobody handled him if they didn't have to, as long as I was there.

As time went on, I started to notice that the people who were most vocal about my little Merlin being "a bad cat" seemed to resent working with *most* of the cats that came in. Cats tend to behave unpredictably in a veterinary setting; they can get frightened or stressed much more easily than many dogs do; most humans can't read their body language as easily; and unlike dogs, they are not typically bred or conditioned to be *obedient*. I believe this is the key point. *Obedience.*

In my experience and observation, the majority of people working in U.S. animal hospitals are confirmed "dog people" who are used to telling patients what to do and having their commands obeyed. You don't typically get this with cats, and when the schedule is crazy and time is of the essence, a patient who readily does what you tell them to do can feel like a godsend, while another who screams and tries to slap you while you're trying to examine them can come close to sending you over the edge sometimes. I get it, but that doesn't make it an acceptable prejudice for any veterinary professional to adopt, and I advise all cat caregivers to satisfy themselves that their own vet clinic has some genuine "cat whisperers" on the job and to learn these staff members' names. (These special people are often more easily found at feline-exclusive veterinary hospitals where cats are *everything* they do, and the level of medical expertise in treating cats like cats rather than "small dogs" tends to be much better at these specialty hospitals, as well.)

I don't mean to imply (and it should not be inferred) that cats are necessarily subjected to abuse in hospitals by overstressed veterinary professionals who may dislike working with them, but cats and dogs alike undoubtedly *know* when a human dislikes them (or having to handle them), and their experience at the vet clinic will feel better or worse, accordingly. Would *you* like to go to a medical appointment if you had a very strong feeling that the nurse or doctor there had a personal dislike for you, or didn't want to have to touch you?

Along with a widespread but clearly erroneous belief that the procedure keeps cats in their homes, these are a few of the reasons that declawing has been supported and endorsed by so many veterinary professionals for so long, despite its *blatant* violation of the Veterinary Oath to "prevent and relieve animal suffering". On quite a few occasions, I heard co-workers expressing relief that the cat who'd just swatted them had only had "Q-tip paws" due to having been previously declawed- and this sentiment could even come from people who claimed not to be in favor of the procedure.

Declawing began to become commonplace in the 1950s (ironically, at approximately the same time the Veterinary Oath was created) after the invention of commercial cat litters which led more people to start keeping their cats indoors, but before that it's believed that the practice originated with dogfighting rings using cats as "bait" animals to get their dogs amped up for fights. (Tail docking and ear cropping in canines have also been traced back to this brutal blood sport and were only later adopted as cosmetic "breed standards" by the dog-fancy community and the American Kennel Club.)18

In November 1952, a DVM by the name of A.G. Misener in Chicago, IL wrote a letter to the Journal of the American Veterinary Medical Association (JAVMA) describing in detail a procedure he'd been doing at his hospital for "several years" and which he referred to as "removal of claws in the domestic cat". 19 (This is, to my knowledge, the earliest known documentation of a licensed veterinarian performing a feline declaw procedure.) In the letter, Misener does not state where he got the idea for this procedure, but it was known by law enforcement and animal welfare advocates at the time that dogfighters would remove the claws of the "bait" animals themselves to prevent undue injury to their fighting dogs until they were *ready* for them to get injured. (And this amounted to torturing the cats before throwing them to their deaths, as well.) With such a dark and cruel history as this, why would "your other family doctor" ever recommend such a thing? Well, Misener *did* have a lot to say about *that:*

"In the city, (cats) sometimes present a serious problem to the owner when the habit of sharpening their claws becomes destructive and some fine article of upholstered furniture is used as a scratching post. Recent reports by the medical profession which have appeared in the press on the dangers of 'cat scratch fever' have also alarmed some cat owners." (Yes, "cat scratch fever" is real, but cat parents stand a better chance of catching it from the fleas *on* their cats than from the cats themselves, and keeping your cat free of fleas is far better protection against infection than declawing is!)

He goes on to say: "For several years in our practice, where the feline pet has become destructive, we have recommended and performed the surgical removal of the claws. This is a relatively simple procedure and, we believe, a practical measure. The owner is always warned that the cat should not be allowed to live outside after this operation, as it will not be able to climb trees or defend itself against other animals. A general anesthetic is administered, usually pentobarbital sodium, intravenously. The feet are thoroughly cleansed with a suitable antiseptic, and a tourniquet is applied proximal to the paw. An autoclaved Resco nail trimmer is used to excise the extended claw at its junction with the terminal phalanx. It is important that all of the corium be excised, otherwise a rudimentary claw will regenerate in a few weeks. A sterile dressing saturated with a crystalline potassium penicillin solution is applied, and the extremity is bandaged with gauze and covered with adhesive tape. The tourniquet is then removed and the bandage left for ninety-six hours. Very little hemorrhage is encountered at the time of surgery and the cat does not seem to evidence

pain during the healing process, which is usually complete at
the end of the ninety-six hours."[20]

For a bit of context here, readers should remember that in the
1950's, it was not universally believed among members of the medical
community that even *human infants* feel pain, so it's perhaps
unsurprising that a DVM at that time could genuinely believe a cat
would not feel pain from having all of their toes amputated. But
Misener's description of his methods and procedure from those "dark
ages" is disturbingly consistent with the way declaw surgery is still
performed today, by and large. The anesthetic and antibiotic drugs used
may be a bit more modern and sophisticated, and in many (though
not all) hospitals, there is a greater degree of patient monitoring and
supportive care; pain control medication is generally given.

But the "Resco nail trimmer" that Misener refers to using is still
extremely common among many practitioners despite the development
of newer techniques using scalpels or lasers, and is exactly what it
sounds like: a crude "guillotine style" pet nail trimmer which was never
intended or manufactured for use as a surgical instrument (and I have
written more than once to the manufacturer to ask why they have never
bothered to denounce the deliberate misuse of their product in this
way. I have never received a reply.) The "Resco method" is still favored
by older DVMs and those who want to save money on (considerably
more expensive) scalpel blades, and never mind the fact that it tends
to *crush* the ends of the bones as it cuts through them while at the
same time failing to precisely excise the germinating cells in the nail bed
which are responsible for claw regrowth. The Resco method virtually
ensures that the patient will have a more difficult recovery and a greater
chance of long-term chronic pain due to bone fragments left behind
and/or the claws regenerating into huge ingrown corkscrews beneath
the skin.

And on the subject of pain control, the American Association of Feline Practitioners notes that "with 20 studies assessing different analgesics, there has been no success in determining a suitable analgesic to meet the pain needs of onychectomy (declaw) patients...No clearly superior analgesic treatment was identified, no single agent was found to be effective, and insufficient evidence exists to support the success or failure of a multimodal analgesic approach. The need for analgesia was observed as long as 12 days postoperatively, yet there are no studies assessing pain beyond this time frame, and most patients go without analgesia, sometimes immediately postoperatively and sometimes after only a few days of analgesia."[21]

There is a great deal more I could say about declawing, and about the reasons why it is in my estimation the single biggest and best indicator of a "profits before patients" mentality in a veterinary hospital, but I will leave that for later in my story.

At the time I was describing, my experience with it would still be fairly limited. Dr. F. had educated her client base very well, and there was little to no demand for the new surgical service Dr. G. was now selling. I believe the first cat he declawed at our hospital was one of his pre-existing patients from his mobile practice. He invited everyone on the staff who was able to stop what they were doing to crowd into the surgery suite to watch the procedure, so that he could prove to us all that "it's not as bad as you've heard". I remember at least one co-worker- one of the kennel staff- who refused to watch, saying she'd witnessed the procedure being done at one of her previous jobs and she could still hear the cat's toe bones and claws clinking against the metal bowl they were tossed into after being summarily chopped off. (In 2023, Rhode Island Senator Melissa Murray, who has sponsored a bill to ban declawing in her state, described an identical scene to *The Providence Journal,* adding: "I assisted with one declawing (when I was a veterinary technician). It was my first and last. It was quite gruesome."[22]

In some ways, I'm ashamed to admit that the first declawing I witnessed was not my last. It certainly was not pleasant, but I had expected it to be much bloodier than it was. Through the magic of the tourniquet that was applied to each of the cat's forelimbs in turn, Dr. G. made all of us who were watching almost forget that *without* it, the patient could have been dead in mere minutes from blood loss consistent with multiple digital amputations. As he worked, he told us that it was important to complete the amputations, suture the toe stumps, and bandage the paw as quickly as possible, because the tourniquet itself was dangerous to the limb the longer it was left in place. (Of course, the faster the doctor tries to be while disarticulating the claws, the greater chance that not all of the claw-germinating cells will be removed cleanly, thus creating a postsurgical complication. It is a fundamentally flawed procedure, harmful no matter how one looks at it.)

There was no clinking of bones and claws in a metal bowl for me to hear; they were laid neatly and quietly on a piece of gauze instead, and with no more blood on them than is typically seen on a lost baby tooth, in kittens and puppies as well as humans. What I *do* remember hearing is the *snap, crack, pop* sound of the nail trimmer going through the bones, but it wasn't very loud. Truthfully, it didn't sound much different from when we used the nail trimmers for their *intended* purpose of simply trimming nails humanely.

The bones in cats' paws are so small and delicate.

The whole thing was over quicker than most surgeries I'd watched or assisted with thus far, and the cat emerged from anesthesia smoothly and without incident.... *that* time. I couldn't stay in the treatment area for long afterward to observe the patient because I was still splitting my weeks between the reception desk and "the back" (I was destined never to take on full-time technician duties at that job), but I supposed I'd seen what there was to see. I didn't like it, and I didn't like that our hospital was going to be doing it now.... but maybe Dr. G. was right; maybe it *wasn't* quite as bad as I'd heard.

At any rate, if I was going to continue working in animal hospitals, I knew I was going to have to get used to it, because it was the status quo to which Dr. F. had been a notable exception. I still very much needed my job. And so I compromised myself again. I told myself that the good I could still do for animals probably outweighed the unfortunate cases where I would be forced to do harm. I took comfort in the fact that none of "our" longtime clients seemed to want their cats declawed simply because it was now being offered, and it stayed rare enough at our hospital for me to mostly avoid being directly involved with it.

And before long, there would be other problems demanding my attention.

CHAPTER FOUR

Jessica had been continuing to gradually play a larger and larger role in the hospital and to be treated with greater and greater deference by many staff members, until one day I heard someone refer to her as "head tech". That was news to me; if she'd actually been given the degree of authority that she liked to pretend she had, I hadn't gotten the memo. I still could see no evidence that she was qualified for such a position. Her tendency to leave tasks unfinished or undocumented had not improved, and she was less and less of a "team player" as each day went by, throwing her weight around more and more to get her own way.

It was beginning to be obvious to everyone (seemingly *except* Dr. G. and Shelly) that nearly every time there was an interpersonal problem among staff members, Jessica seemed to be involved in it in some way. Every time a vital tool like a stethoscope or an opthalmoscope couldn't be found when needed, it seemed that Jessica had been the one who'd been asked to put it back where it belonged, and who had to retrace her steps to find it. There were a lot of little things like this adding up, but I was beginning to realize that Dr. G. either couldn't see it or didn't want to. Whenever anyone brought a concern to him, he promised he would speak to Jessica about it, but nothing was changing,

One of the more serious and concerning issues I was noticing was that the controlled drug log had been looking sloppier than ever lately, with some entries barely legible and others scribbled out and re-written, and the drug inventory in the lockbox wasn't always matching the logged amounts at the end of the day. While I had been managing most of the hospital's inventory since long before Dr. G. took over, the controlled drug inventory and ordering had always been handled by Roberta or Dr. F. themselves. Now, however, that responsibility had fallen to "the head tech", who was always acting unconcerned when these discrepancies were noticed and remarked upon- usually by me, but often by one of the associate doctors, as well.

I was annoyed at how many evenings I was finding myself staying late, trying to decipher everyone's hurried scribbles in the drug log and adding the numbers up again and again, trying to make them balance with the amounts of the medications that I could see in front of me. This probably should have been "the head tech's" duty, but it was part of the general end-of-day closing checklist considered to be everyone's responsibility. I just seemed to be the only one who cared about its accuracy.

I reminded Jessica again and again that she also had to log "hub remainders" and make sure everyone else was logging them as well. A hub remainder is the tiny amount of an injectable drug that will always be wasted per injection because it remains in the hub of the needle when the plunger of the syringe is fully depressed. Typically about 0.065-0.070ml per injection[23], these really add up over time when not accounted for. I knew that if any authorities ever asked to see our records, there was a good chance the hospital could be shut down over something like this, but I was beginning to believe it had essentially already been lost, and I had been detaching myself emotionally from the place for some time. It felt like a sinking ship. I wanted out, and I started quietly scanning classified ads and Craig's List, watching for openings at other animal hospitals in town. And then the younger of my two cats grew a suspicious mass on his shoulder blade.

Injection-induced sarcomas in cats were very much a concern of mine at that time since one of our clinic cats had suffered from the condition and had to be euthanized. Originally termed Vaccine Induced Sarcoma (VIS) and recognized as a concern since 1991[24], these aggressive tumors have been linked *primarily* to feline vaccines (the rabies vaccine and feline leukemia/FeLV vaccine in particular), but other types of injections such as corticosteroid injections have also been implicated. A very small number of cases have also been linked to microchip implantation. Now termed Feline Injection Site Sarcomas (FISS), they are still not very well understood, but they are the reason why vaccine protocol recommendations have been gradually changing to tailor vaccine administration to cats' individual lifestyles and risk of exposure to various diseases. It's also the reason that vaccine manufacturer Boehringer Ingelheim (previously Merial) created their PureVax brand of feline vaccines free of the chemical adjuvants which boost efficacy, but which have been particularly implicated in the formation of these (usually fatal) sarcomas in cats. It's the reason for the recommendation that all vaccine sites on a cat's body be recorded and that whenever possible, the same vaccines should be given in the same locations so that it can be known *which* vaccine might be to blame for a tumor forming. Likewise, it's why another recommendation is for vaccines and other injections be given to cats as low as possible on a limb, as far away from the body as possible, in the event that the limb needs to be amputated due to a sarcoma forming at the injection site.

Your vet never mentioned any of this to you? Of course not. They don't want to scare anyone away from getting the time-honored "annual vaccine package" for their pet which has long been the financial cornerstone of the modern veterinary practice. I don't want to scare anyone away from it entirely either; vaccines *are* an important part of keeping companion animals healthy, and I believe cats and dogs should always be vaccinated against common and devastating diseases which pose a risk to them. But what has traditionally been done- giving *every* vaccine *every* year- is medically unnecessary and too much, and this is finally beginning to be recognized and acknowledged within the profession. This is true for dogs as well as for cats, since in addition to feline injection site sarcomas, overvaccination can result in increased risk of adverse reactions and anaphylaxis in both species. An excellent guide for pet caregivers on this topic entitled "Preventing Unnecessary Overvaccination In Dogs and Cats" has been published online by

Family Veterinary Mobile Clinic, which serves the Sanford and Southern Pines areas of North Carolina.

My beautiful, two-year-old black cat Malachai (who I'd *also* adopted from the clinic in order to keep him out of the high-kill city shelter) had gotten a methylprednisolone injection for skin allergies recently and now had a firm, flat mass under the skin of his right shoulder blade. It was in a place where he'd also received some vaccines in the past, and I was worried. I brought him in with me one day to have one of the doctors look at it. Dr. G. took a cursory glance and said emphatically that it should be removed as soon as possible, so I agreed to go ahead with it that very day.

It was a typical day- a little better than typical, actually. We weren't quite as slammed as we normally were, and I thought it would be a good day to get this taken care of. It was assumed that I would be assisting with the surgery, because that's the way it always tended to be when a staff pet needed treatment; we always just acted as the nurses for our own animals. It was assumed the pets would be better behaved and less stressed that way, and of course most of us *wanted* to be involved directly in our own pet's treatment. So we prepped my baby for surgery.

A fairly standard practice when anesthetizing cats at our hospital was known as "tanking down". This meant the cat was placed into an "isoflurane tank" which consisted of a small fishtank-like chamber connected to the anesthesia machine. The cat was placed in the tank, the tank was pumped full of isoflurane gas anesthesia, and the cat lapsed into unconsciousness without any staff member needing to exercise any manual restraint. This "touchless" technique was the preferred method for sedating cats and had been thus since Dr. F.'s days of running the hospital. (I would later learn that this method is considered less than kind by many practitioners who work exclusively with cats; it's slower to take effect than injecting the anesthetic by IV, and many are disturbed by the contortions the cats will typically go through in the tank as they succumb to the anesthesia, interpreting these as signs of distress and comparing it to euthanasia by gas chamber (at least from the cat's perspective). I was assured by every doctor I'd worked with that the nature of the inhaled drug made all the difference and "tanked" cats were "just fighting to stay awake", not struggling to breathe. I'm not sure how common this method is today, but in 2001 it was certainly not *un*common.)

We would use the Isotank to "knock them down" and make them easy to handle, at which point the doctor would usually give an additional dose of injectable anesthesia since the isoflurane was very quickly dispersed once the tank was opened, and the cats would regain consciousness rapidly otherwise. We would then intubate and continue prepping the patient for surgery.

We'd gotten to this stage with Malachai when I noticed that his breathing had slowed considerably- beyond what seemed normal- and I alerted Dr. G. He stopped what he was doing to watch Malachai closely, and soon determined that he had actually gone into respiratory arrest. The next thing I knew, I was in a nightmare in which my child's life was hanging in the balance and I was responsible for breathing for him- gently squeezing oxygen into his lungs from the machine's reservoir bag for 20 minutes- while Dr. G. worked to clear the anesthesia from his system and revive him. We never actually began the surgery to remove the mass. (Four months after this incident, it would disappear on its own entirely, never to return. This taught me a vivid and lasting lesson about making too-hasty decisions regarding anesthetic and surgical procedures.)

Dr. G. told me that Malachai had an abnormal sensitivity to common anesthetic drugs (NO TELAZOL OR KETAMINE! was emblazoned in huge lettering across the front of his medical record now) and could "never be safely sedated" again. For months I believed that he'd simply had a close call which had been impossible to predict, and we'd been very lucky to pull him back from the brink. But other doctors at other hospitals who subsequently looked over his chart told me that the dose of Telazol he was given during this event (1mg per pound of body weight of 12.6 pounds) was too high on top of the inhalation anesthesia already administered in the Isotank. And this is assuming that what Dr. G. wrote in his record after the fact was the actual amount of the drug administered to my baby- I'll never know *that* with any degree of certainty since I didn't watch him draw it up. He wrote that notation *after* he nearly killed Malachai- not before.

I'll also never know if Dr. G. was simply distracted when drawing up the drugs that that day by the chaos that he typically invited into the hospital, or whether something else was going on. I'll never know (for sure) whether the missing drugs that couldn't be accounted for had anything to do with his grave error in either calculating or measuring my cat's anesthesia dose. But I *do* know that rather than admit his mistake, he was prepared to let me believe that I could never allow my cat to be sedated or anesthetized for any treatment ever again. In fact, he deliberately misled me to believe this.

This could have seriously compromised Malachai's future healthcare- and could potentially even have resulted in his life being needlessly cut short- had I never taken him to another veterinarian and had continued believing that anesthesia was not an option for him (even if lifesaving surgery was needed).

I also know that one day, Dr. G. gave me a ride home after we'd both ended up staying at the hospital late, and I noticed used syringes scattered all over the floor of his car, which seemed a bit strange. Had he been vaccinating animals in his car? That was what I unthinkingly assumed at the time, and I still suppose that's possible... *maybe.*

But that wasn't the only thing that was hard to explain. There was also the way that Jessica-on repeated occasions- would "accidentally" lock her dog in the business office (where the controlled drug lockbox was kept) and ask various co-workers to try to pick the lock to get in before her dog began to panic. (Soon, I'd put two and two together and realize she was trying to establish witnesses to the fact that this or that person was *capable* of getting in there and accessing the drugs.) There were also the hours she would spend in there by herself, with no one else on staff having the slightest idea what she could be doing in there for so long. There's the way she drew me aside one day, expressing concern over how "stressed and depressed" I'd been seeming, and telling me that she thought I should try one of her prescription antidepressants- pressuring me a little to take one, in fact. (I refused, but it was another thing that would soon make a lot more sense in hindsight.)

Again, there were a lot of little things adding up, but the big picture didn't come into focus until after a number of us on the staff were rounded up and told that we would be required to submit to drug testing if we wanted to keep our jobs. We were told that the DEA *had* finally taken notice of the sheer quantity of ketamine our hospital had been ordering recently and we were being threatened with an investigation, so Shelly was conducting an internal investigation first. (I now doubt that this was strictly true; I doubt the DEA would have waited to investigate if they had noticed such huge discrepancies themselves. I believe this was merely a ruse to explain and justify Shelly's actions to the staff.)

So, it was finally being openly acknowledged that controlled drugs were missing and it was a problem, but the blame was falling on the shoulders of everyone who *wasn't* directly responsible for ordering them or entering them into the hospital inventory. Everyone who *wasn't* ingratiating themselves to Dr. G. and Shelly. Everyone who was making dissenting noises about The New Way.

I was going to have to try to defend myself against implications that I was responsible for the very problem I'd been trying to call attention to in recent months, and I was tired. I was tired of the tension, tired of the politics, tired of our staff focusing on everything *but* the patients, seemingly. I was disgusted and saddened by what I'd seen my beloved animal hospital become under Dr. G's dubious "leadership". I submitted to the drug testing- albeit with the counsel of a lawyer friend- and though I knew the results would exonerate me, I also knew that my time there was done. When my employers further demanded that I submit to an interview with a private investigator they'd hired and my lawyer friend advised *against* it because in his estimation it sounded "like a set-up", I was told that my refusal amounted to my resignation. It was a "mutual decision" for me to leave- which made me ineligible to apply for unemployment, but I hardly cared, because I was finally, sadly, *glad* to be leaving by that point.

A few months later I would run into a former co-worker who had also been among the ones targeted by the internal investigation- the very same one who'd refused to watch that first declaw surgery Dr. G. had demonstrated for us, in fact. She told me that she and several others who'd been rounded up that day had all either ended up resigning or being let go from the hospital after me, and that one of the others had confided in *her* before leaving that she'd inadvertently walked in on Jessica and Dr. G. in a very compromising position which seemed to indicate a sexual relationship between them. (After witnessing this, my other former co-worker had apparently found herself to be Jessica's next target, but decided to leave on her own terms rather than wait for Jessica to set her up to take a fall, the way she'd done to me.)

There was now nobody left at the hospital who hadn't been brought to heel under Dr. G., Jessica, and Shelly (who *must* have at least suspected some of what her husband and her employee were appearing to be up to together by this time). They'd successfully gotten rid of everyone who wasn't willing to look the other way and mind their own business, and even some people who *were* willing, for good measure. And all I could think about when I heard all this was- who was looking out for the patients there now? If Jessica and Dr. G. were showing such poor judgement as to be (allegedly) groping each other right there in the hospital in the middle of the workday when anyone could walk in on them, then what was going on in their heads while they were also (often literally) holding animals' lives in their hands? Was *that* the reason Malachai had nearly died? Would something similar happen to someone else's cat or dog? Would anyone catch it in time, the next time?

These questions gnawed at me until I decided to contact the Georgia State Board of Veterinary Medicine and tell them what I knew about the goings-on at that animal hospital. State veterinary boards are the only thing we have in the U.S. approaching a governing body with the authority to discipline bad veterinarians. They issue a DVM's license to practice and are the only entities I know of with the power to revoke it- although, this rarely happens. These boards are generally made up of fellow veterinarians, and their overwhelming tendency is to give their fellow veterinarians the benefit of the doubt when faced with accusations of wrongdoing, while being loath to dictate how their colleagues can or cannot practice veterinary medicine. (This is a problem. A governing body or authority which shies away from telling those *under* its authority what they can and cannot do is not a very effective one. Nor is one that tries hard not to see it when one of "their own" has become a bad apple.)

I wrote a long and detailed letter describing everything I'd seen and heard- from the poorly kept controlled drug log to the way Dr. G. had on several occasions written antibiotic prescriptions for his employees when they were bitten by animals at work. (It was and is, of course, highly illegal for veterinarians to prescribe medications for human beings, but this was easier and more cost effective for Dr. G. than paying workers' compensation for them to be treated by an M.D. He would simply invent a fictional large dog for the bitten employee and write the prescription for the "dog"). I admitted in my letter to the board that I lacked any hard proof, but felt certain that if they inspected the hospital themselves, they would find evidence to support my claims. I couldn't imagine that Jessica and Dr. G. would clean up their act before such an inspection could take place- after all, why *would* they, now?

But the reply I got from the state board a few weeks later was disappointing. It said that an investigation had been conducted and Dr. G. had been required to pay a small fine, but I was not given any further details. I couldn't believe that they couldn't find enough violations throughout the hospital to pull his license, but I could imagine how the conversation between Dr. G. and the board-dispatched inspector had probably gone: Dr. G. would have referred to me as a "disgruntled employee" who was "exaggerating" or "outright lying" out of "spite", and I wouldn't have been surprised if that was all he needed to say.

I took a short break from working in veterinary medicine after leaving that first hospital, opting for a comparatively low-stress job in retail while I reassessed my life. It was a huge relief for a while to go to work each day knowing that no matter what happened during my shift, it wasn't going to be a matter of life and death. I didn't have to exercise such exhausting vigilance over every little thing I did- or every little thing my co-workers did, either- because no cat or dog was going to suffer because of someone neglecting to do something correctly. For a few months, it felt almost like being on vacation in comparison.

But before too long, I began to remember what the other side of that feeling was like: the depressing *meaninglessness* of what I was doing now was familiar in a way I'd never wanted to feel again, and I started to miss working in a veterinary setting. At the same time, my husband and I were falling in love with the city of New Orleans, where we'd gone on one of our (rare) vacations and where we thought we wanted to relocate. I started looking at Craig's List ads for apartments and job listings in New Orleans- idly and casually at first, and then more carefully. When I came across an ad for a feline-exclusive veterinary hospital in New Orleans' Lower Garden District which was looking to hire a technician with "no license required", it seemed almost like a sign. I sent them my resume and got an interview.

And so it looked like we'd be taking a road trip; nearly 500 miles from Atlanta to New Orleans is certainly the farthest I've ever traveled for a job interview! Fortunately, it was easy to get time off from my retail position on short notice, and we made the trip into a mini vacation that also included apartment hunting. It would be a whirlwind of a week that would end up impacting my life in ways I could never have imagined.

CHAPTER FIVE

My family- myself, my husband, and our two cats- moved to New Orleans in the late spring of 2002 and I started my new job at the feline-exclusive veterinary hospital the very day after we arrived. I was delighted by the fact that we were going to be living within walking distance of my job and I would get to enjoy the scent of jasmine in bloom on my way to work.

I carefully wended my way around stacks of boxes all over our new apartment to get dressed and ready for my first shift- which couldn't wait for us to take a few days to unpack and settle in; the hospital needed me ASAP. I should have seen this as a red flag, but at the time, I'd seen it as working in my favor, since I knew I couldn't count on a good reference from my previous veterinary position! I remember being worried about exactly what I would tell the manager (who I'll call "Tanya") in my interview about how and why I'd left that job, but as it turned out, she never asked me for many details. I think I said something about the clinic changing hands and the new owners getting rid of the old staff to bring in their own people- which was certainly true, after all.

What sticks in my mind more clearly about that interview is that she asked me "How do you feel about pregnant spays?" While this wasn't a question I'd anticipated, it didn't really strike me as strange. I'd never had to assist with an ovariohysterectomy on a pregnant patient before, but I knew it was done routinely enough, particularly in shelter medicine, and was considered a higher risk surgery but still reasonably safe with proper monitoring and support. So that's what I said.

"Oh, good," Tanya replied. "Because we've had a couple of techs we've had to let go in the past because they didn't believe in it, and they were telling clients not to have it done for their cats." She went on to tell me that they couldn't have anyone but the doctors advising clients on whether surgery was right for them or their cats, and she hoped I could understand that. "And no contradicting or undermining the opinions of the doctors in front of clients."

"Uh... of course!" I said quickly. "I wouldn't presume to!"

How those words would come back to haunt me.

But Tanya wasn't finished. "Especially when it's just your own personal beliefs and not veterinary science. Spaying a pregnant cat isn't wrong just because someone is 'pro-life', so we can't have our employees telling people that it is!" It was clear that this topic made her angry, despite her professional demeanor.

"Oh... Really, that was why?" It was out of my mouth before I could think twice. "Well, I'm pro-choice so *that* wouldn't be an issue for me." When that earned me a smile from Tanya, I knew the interview was going my way. At its conclusion, she hired me on the spot and told me that as soon as I could relocate permanently to New Orleans, they would need me to start. I thanked her and told her that as soon as I left the interview, my husband and I had a list of apartments to go and see.

We ended up choosing the first one we'd looked at after dutifully viewing them all, and everything fell into place so quickly that it could have been fated to happen. It wasn't until the long drive back to Atlanta to start packing (and give notice at the retail job) that I had time to replay the interview in my mind and think about how it had gone. I felt like I'd made a pretty good impression on Tanya, and my instinct told me her opinion would carry considerable weight at this new job. I hoped it meant I was off to a good start.

It was only then that I realized she hadn't asked me how I felt about declawing.

Before the time I'd put in working for Dr. F. and Dr. G. in Atlanta, I'd been aware there were such things as animal hospitals which would only see cats, and back then I thought it was "kind of snooty of them", as I can recall once saying to my husband. In the same way I'd once thought that declawing cats couldn't really be that bad, I thought a hospital dedicated exclusively to cats couldn't really be that necessary. There certainly weren't very many of them, so wasn't it just self-evident?

I made that observation circa 1995 (before working in vet med and before I became a cat person!). In 2023, of the estimated 28,000-30,000 veterinary hospitals in the United States[25], only approximately 600 of them were seeing cats exclusively.[26] Feline specialty veterinary practices are clearly still a niche market, for a certain kind of discriminating cat caretaker. Before the early 1970s, it seems, they were virtually unheard of. [27]

The current owner of one of the country's first cat-only hospitals to appear back in 1973- The Cat Practice of New York City- told Petful.com in January 2023 that feline specialty practices are more popular in areas "where there's a higher (pet) cat population. In the big city, there's a higher percentage of apartment dwellers, and that usually means a lot more cat people...(and) if you're a cat-only person, you often take your cat just as seriously as you would a child."[28]

Tanya had told me in my interview that this was the kind of client that "Dr. C." had in mind when he'd decided to get *an additional certification* (she emphasized the words) beyond his veterinary medical degree so he could specialize in feline medicine. He was in fact the only board-certified specialist in feline medicine practicing in the entire southeast U.S., she said.

Of course I had been duly impressed to hear this, and it had made me want the job even more. I considered myself one of "those" cat people by now, and while I still liked dogs and other animals too, I was excited by the opportunity to learn more in-depth about conditions and problems specific to cats, which I believed would make me a better adoptive "parent" to my own. It would be nice to be able to go home to them at night without smelling like dogs, too- that couldn't be denied! I looked forward to working with my favorite kind of patient all day every day, and to a working environment that promised to be *all about cats* in every way.

So I was a little taken aback when I finally started getting to work with and to know Dr. C. a little. He was also a partner at another animal hospital in town, a mixed practice (meaning they saw both cats and dogs) and so he was really only there at the cat clinic on a part-time basis. His associate- a perky young DVM I'll call "Dr. D."- was the one I met and worked with first because it was she who really "held down the fort" at the feline practice on a day-to-day basis, seeing most of the appointments and handling most of the medical cases. Dr. C. would often split his day between both hospitals, but I was told he greatly preferred working at the feline hospital, and was trying to make it successful enough so that he could sell his share of the other clinic to his partner and be at the feline practice exclusively. (In retrospect, this is something else I should have seen as a red flag, considering my *last* experience with a vet who harbored a lot of strong ambitions for the financial success of his practice.)

Dr. C. did not strike me as a cat person at all. He had a big, booming voice that he seemed unable to modulate most of the time, even when a patient was obviously tense and stressed. He was prone to making abrupt or sudden movements with a brisk and hurried manner overall, and that tended to have an even worse effect on some cats' tolerance level and patience with us. He had a tendency to *pat* cats the way one might pat a dog- something that most cats don't usually appreciate, at least not when coming from someone other than "their" human. He would do this while talking a mile a minute to the cat's caregiver and without paying any attention to the cat's body language. I could certainly see why most of our clients preferred to see Dr. D. She was everything he was not in the exam room: a soft-spoken, calming presence who communicated her willingness to listen to the client at every step of the way, and who could literally get a fractious patient to eat from the palm of her hand.

Most of the staff preferred to work with Dr. D. as well. For one thing, she wasn't above rolling up her sleeves and washing a bowl or a litterpan once in a while, if she needed a clean one right then and happened to be the closest one to the sink. She treated the techs, receptionists, and kennel staff a little more like her equals than Dr. C. did (and perhaps more so than most of the doctors I'd worked with thus far). But she also seemed to enjoy explaining things to us- not just *how* to do something, but *why* it was done that way; not just what to watch for in a patient we were monitoring, but also what the patient would likely be experiencing, based on what's known about the same conditions in human medicine.

She impressed upon me the almost *sacred* nature of what we were doing when we put cats under anesthesia and opened their bodies to the air: "We take them right to the threshold of death every day. And then our job is to bring them back."

I felt I was learning a great deal from her- more than I'd even hoped. She was also an exceedingly *cheerful* person whose upbeat mood was usually much better for staff morale than Dr. C.'s frequent impatience and irritability. Generally speaking, everyone expected the day to be better on a "Dr. D. Day" than we did on a "Dr. C. Day".

But for all of that, he certainly seemed to command the genuine respect of the whole senior staff- from Tanya, Dr. D., and our one other DVM (a "Dr. K." who wasn't far from going on maternity leave and who worked only on Dr. D.'s weekly day off and alternating Saturdays) on down to the head tech "Alyssa", who lived in a studio apartment on the floor above the hospital and was on-call 24 hours a day. All of them would refer to Dr. C. as "a genius", "a brilliant man", and in other similarly glowing terms. All of them seemed quick to make excuses for his often-brusque treatment of both staff and patients alike, usually to the effect that he was just such a *busy* man with so many demands on his time. In addition to running one hospital and being partner at another, he was also a lecturer for Pfizer (later Zoetis) Animal Health and the

Merial corporation, frequently asked to speak at various veterinary schools, conferences or events. He couldn't always be expected to take the extra time necessary to "sweet talk" a cat in an appointment, but *clearly*, he loved them. Why else would he dedicate his career and his entire practice to them? He might not always be very sensitive to the needs or feelings of his employees, either, but most of the (100% female) staff seemed to think this was simply "typical of a man" to a certain extent. (This struck me as an off-putting, antiquated attitude and I did not agree with it. I half-wondered if it was due to the culture of New Orleans, which *is* antiquated in many ways and still extremely influenced by the Catholic Church.)

There was one other tech who never volunteered excuses for Dr. C., though. "Michelle" took me under her wing when I started and helped me further my on-the-job training, which I still felt I very much needed. I'd only had limited time and experience working as a tech back in Atlanta, and this hospital had more advanced equipment than I'd used before. They also typically carried medical cases much farther and pursued more aggressive treatment plans than I'd seen any DVM do before, so there was much that was brand new to me here, and I was extremely uncomfortable in the beginning with just how much Dr. C. expected me to be able to do flawlessly, right away. (It wasn't just me; he expected the same from *all* new trainees, and would often get pushy about forcing people to start doing tasks they didn't feel ready for- like restraining a cat for jugular venipuncture, for example, or perhaps placing an IV catheter or administering a radial nerve block during surgical prep. These were sensitive operations requiring a highly skilled technique, and I simply could not see it as being in any way good for patient care (let alone staff morale and mental health) for us to be pushed into attempting them for the first time under duress and in haste, and Michelle agreed with me.) Michelle and I soon found we had a lot in common, and she became my favorite other tech with whom to work.

It was Michelle who told me that not too long before I'd started working there, Dr. C. had opened a *second* cat clinic on New Orleans' West Bank, across the Mississippi River from our Uptown location, but had been forced to close the second hospital due to a lack of support from the suburban blue-collar neighborhood where he'd misguidedly chosen to put it. (Remember the conventional wisdom about the kinds of neighborhoods where feline-only veterinary hospitals tend to thrive?)

His original plan, she said, had been to eventually expand to even *more* locations around town, like a few other DVMs he knew who were building multiple branches of their practices locally. Those other vets were running mixed practices however, seeing mostly dogs, and the market for their services was much bigger. Ultimately, he'd decided to focus his energy and resources on the single cat hospital in the heart of the city, and to make it that much *more* successful- as well as exclusive, "for people who really care about their cats."

Michelle also agreed with me that Dr. C. wasn't much of a cat person in reality, though, and told me she thought the real reason he'd wanted to specialize in feline medicine was because he harbored an actual *dis*like for dogs. "He hates having to see dogs, that's why he wants out of the other hospital partnership," she elaborated. "He hates birds too- he says birds are 'disgusting dinosaur things' that shouldn't even be alive at the same time as human beings."

"*Wow.*"

"Yeah, it's like cats are just the animals that annoy him the *least*. And it doesn't hurt that he knows he can get what he calls 'crazy cat ladies' to pay higher fees here than at any other animal hospital in town." (Here, I should state that I don't believe and do not wish to imply that this attitude is commonplace among feline specialist DVMs; I believe the majority of them have chosen their specialty for the right reasons, and if their fees are higher than the mixed practices in their area, it's legitimately due to their greater level of expertise with cats rather than simple avarice. But despite the veterinary profession's adamant insistence that "nobody goes into vet med to get rich", my experience has taught me that- just as clients so often suspect- there are indeed at least a *few* DVMs who do exactly that.)

Also like me (and unlike most of the rest of the staff), Michelle disapproved of declawing, and she told me that Dr. C. had declawed all of his own cats over the years, as well as the clinic cat Missy, after she'd scratched Tanya one day.

I felt a bit sick when I heard that. Poor Missy was completely bald over the top of her head and had thick scar tissue there. It was believed she'd suffered some kind of chemical burn- possibly as a victim of cruelty- before a client of the hospital had found her and brought her to Dr. C. for emergency treatment. The staff had convinced him to let her live in the hospital after the client funded her recovery but couldn't adopt her; it was believed her odd appearance would be an obstacle to her finding a home through other channels like the local SPCA. After she'd apparently swatted at Tanya one day, though, Dr. C. had gotten angry about it and declawed her almost immediately, saying that he couldn't take a chance on her "injuring a client".

Michelle and I commiserated briefly over that together, as I recall, taking turns stroking Missy's poor little bald head and scratching under her chin. There'd been several other potential solutions to the situation, we agreed- Missy could have been confined to the kennel, where she spent most of her time anyway and where clients generally were not permitted without employee supervision. She could have been re-homed with a staff member or possibly with a client; or she could have been fitted with vinyl claw caps (marketed under such trade names as Soft Paws or Soft Claws). Quite possibly *nothing* really needed to be done- Missy wasn't usually aggressive to people, and we might have never seen behavior like that from her again. But rather than consider all of that, Dr. C. had chosen to cut off all her toes so there could be absolutely no possibility of her ever using her claws again- for *anything*.

It made me want to cry for her, and it made me far less trusting of Dr. C., and more trusting of my own intuition. I'd just *known* he wasn't really a true cat person!

As a popular saying and a song both state, "two out of three ain't bad," and out of the three doctors at our hospital, I loved working with two, so I just tried to focus on that. I related more to Dr. D. on a personal level than I did Dr. K.- both because she was a little closer to my own age and because like me, she'd chosen *not* to have children despite being happily married to a man; she and her husband thought of their cats as their children, just like my husband and I thought of ours.

Because of that, I thought I could perceive a difference in the way she would discuss treatment plans with cats' caretakers versus the other doctors. She would routinely center and prioritize *the cats themselves* and their needs rather than those of their caretakers- which was only right in my opinion, and the way I felt *all* veterinarians ideally should be: focused on their *patient*. She seemed better able to get inside the minds of her feline patients than any other vet I'd known, and she spent more time educating their people about normal and natural feline behavior. She couldn't always persuade the client to accept all her best recommendations, but she always gave it a valiant effort.

Dr. K., on the other hand, was a devoted mom to her human children first and a DVM second, as far as I could see. Her husband was *also* a DVM with his own mixed practice in another part of town, and Dr. K. seemed quite content to be gradually moving her own veterinary career onto the back burner while she raised her kids. In contrast to Dr. D., in the exam room Dr. K. would center and prioritize the client and *their* needs and concerns- whether those concerns were over the amount of the bill, the ease or difficulty of administering a medication or treatment at home, or some other matter. She was the most diligent of all the doctors about getting the client a detailed estimate for anything and everything she was recommending and making certain they were willing to pay for it all, and she was the quickest to amend her treatment plans to accommodate the client's budget and/or level of engagement with their cat at home. She would take it more in stride than either Dr. D. or I would when a cat's caretaker seemed to think of them as "just a cat" rather than a full-fledged member of the family. Listening to her talk about her own family's pets (they had dogs as well as cats), it sounded as though they were thought of in much the same way the family dogs were thought of by my own parents when I was growing up: *kind of like* family members, but not in quite the same way or on quite the same level as the *human* ones were. I couldn't fault Dr. K. for that though, I reasoned; this is after all the way most people tend to think in our society, and it's my personal belief that this tendency is particularly strong in people who have human children.

This was the reason I thought of Dr. D. as more of a kindred spirit, but Dr. K. was still great with the cats- gentle, considerate, attentive, and thorough- and very clearly cared about them a great deal. She was an absolute sweetheart to the support staff on the few days she filled in for Dr. D., and everyone loved her despite her poor time management skills and the way the team would inevitably and invariably "get in the weeds" on "Dr. K. Days".

Where Dr. D. prioritized her patients and Dr. K. prioritized serving their humans, Dr. C.'s first and foremost priority always seemed to be working towards a greater level of success for the hospital. His favorite clients were the ones who he could form some kind of business connection with; the ones he perceived as being able to also help *him* out in some way in exchange for some discount on services or some special "VIP" treatment when they brought their cat to be seen. He was constantly networking, constantly "schmoozing", constantly planning other projects or writing speeches in his head while he saw patients, while he made notes about their cases, while he discussed treatments with their caretakers... and while he was cutting them open in the surgery suite. He seemed to *never* be focused entirely on one patient or thing at a time, giving that cat or that task his entire attention. Like Dr. G. (and countless others), he believed the busier we were, the better, and he would have the receptionists pack the schedule with as many appointments as possible day after day, even when it was already fairly full and the calls coming in were just for annual vaccines and not sick cats that really *needed* to be seen.

I strongly felt that we should always try to leave at least a little wiggle room in the schedule for the inevitable emergencies and unscheduled sick cases that usually came in during the course of a day, but Dr. C. didn't believe in that, just as Dr. G. hadn't.

"We can handle it, I have faith in my crew!" he'd say dismissively, waving at the receptionists to indicate they should go ahead and schedule yet another vaccine appointment. On one occasion, when I actually heard Dr. C. *say* the words "the busier, the better!", I dryly remarked that the busier we were, the more cats must be getting sick or hurt, since that was the nature of a *hospital*. I'd be lying if I said it didn't give me a small measure of satisfaction to see Dr. C.'s face redden ever so slightly at that, and to see him glance quickly and furtively around to be sure no clients had heard me say it.

Because of things like this, I wasn't surprised to learn that my feelings about Dr. C. were apparently somewhat mutual and I was not his favorite tech to work with, just as he wasn't my favorite doctor. That honor went to Alyssa, of course, who had worked for him since she was in high school and who'd already put in a decade there. Alyssa seemed to have the near-supernatural energy level of a young child fed coffee ice cream, and never seemed to bat an eye at the long shifts (10-12 hours was the norm, very often without even a lunch break)- because for her, they never really ended. Whenever the hospital had one or more patients staying overnight, she would do rounds at scheduled intervals, contacting Dr. C. if there was any problem or emergency with a hospitalized patient and administering any feedings, medications, or other treatments the doctor(s) had deemed necessary.

Her small apartment above the hospital had been specially built into its floor plan so that Dr. C. could offer his clients something that even today remains woefully rare in American veterinary medicine: namely, round-the-clock care on the premises, eliminating the need for critical cases to be shuttled to an after-hours emergency hospital for overnight treatment or monitoring and back to the regular attending vet every morning. It was one of the "exclusive perks" of being a client of *his* cat hospital. Strictly speaking, however, no animal hospital which does *not* have trained staff on the premises 24 hours a day should *really* be keeping "hospitalized" patients on the premises during those hours when they will be completely unattended, and the facility *certainly* should not be charging the patient's caretaker for an implied level of care which does not exist in reality.

So, if your pet ever requires (or required in the past) an overnight "hospital" stay, I advise you to question your vet about the level of care and monitoring they will receive (or did receive), particularly if you were (or will be) charged a "hospitalization fee". That was something that Dr. C. never stopped tacking on to invoices for cats going home from overnight visits for medical reasons- even long after both the upstairs apartment and Alyssa herself were gone.

On the Friday morning leading up to the start of Labor Day Weekend 2002, about three months after I'd started at the cat clinic, I was getting ready for work when a story on the local TV news caught my attention. Firefighters were shown rushing to the site of an eight-alarm fire that was threatening to engulf an entire city block in the Lower Garden District, where there were known to be two animal care facilities. When the street name was announced, I felt a sickening shock as I realized the reporter was talking about where both my husband and

I worked. (The other facility mentioned in the report was a boarding kennel and grooming salon for both cats and dogs where my husband had gotten a job soon after I'd started working a few doors down the block.)

I hadn't been scheduled to be there that day until a couple of hours after opening, so when I phoned the hospital to find out the state of things, I hoped intensely (and half expected) that someone would answer just as they always did, and they'd tell me that they were being advised to evacuate patients and staff from the building as a precaution, or something. But the phone just rang and rang endlessly, and the next thing I knew, I was looking at TV footage of the outside of my workplace with thick black smoke billowing from the roof. Then there was an aerial view of the whole block, and I could see huge flames bursting through the roofs of the other businesses and shops not far away. It was a good thing I'd managed to get dressed by this point, because I think at that moment, I simply dropped the phone, burst out of my apartment, and started running.

CHAPTER SIX

The fire swept through the row of century-old-plus buildings in a very short time and ended up completely gutting the entire block of businesses, including both our hospital and the boarding and grooming facility where my husband worked. The firefighters said it must have started very early that morning, and they'd traced it to a stained-glass art studio located in about the middle of the block. It had spread out quickly in both directions through the businesses' shared attic space- which was *supposed* to have dividing fire walls between each, but which several of the businesses had not been keeping up to code. Alyssa and her husband had managed to narrowly escape from their upstairs apartment with their lives, but lost all six of their own cats in the fire, along with all their material belongings.

In addition to theirs, every cat who was boarding in our kennel, every cat who was staying in our hospital ward, and poor little Missy with her bald, chemical-burned little head... all crossed the Rainbow Bridge that day, as well as some of the cats and dogs from the boarding and grooming facility. No human beings were harmed. If the fire had started less than 24 hours later (after the rest of our scheduled boarders would have been dropped off that day for the holiday weekend), the animal death toll at both facilities would have been even higher than it was.

As all of us- staff members from both animal facilities- stood together across the street helplessly watching the block burn, many crying on each other's shoulders, a rainbow actually appeared low in the sky, arching over the blazing rooftops, in the mist generated by the firefighters' hoses. I don't think a single one of us failed to take notice of it.

The cause of the fire was later determined to be arson, with insurance fraud as the suspected motive (although that part was never proven). It was believed by investigators that the intention of the arsonist(s) had only been for the stained-glass studio to burn, not the entire block, but they hadn't anticipated how the fire might spread through the shared attic. The ATF's main suspect in the case fell from a balcony and died not long afterward, and the investigation seemed to stall after that; at any rate, those of us impacted by the fire stopped hearing anything more about it.

I remember being relieved- in a strange way- to know that this horrific tragedy had struck our hospital from outside; that the loss of all those cats could not be laid at the feet of one of our own staff, because the first thought that had shot through my head when I saw the building burning on TV had been: *Did someone forget to turn off the autoclave?* And the second had been: *What about the oxygen tank?* In the short time I'd been working there, I'd already been falling into a habit of trying to double-check that things like that were done at the end of the day, the way I'd been doing back in Atlanta under Dr. G., because it felt necessary to me again in an equally fast-paced and chaotic hospital. But I couldn't double-check *all* the things *all* the time. And what if I'd forgotten something like that *myself*? But I hadn't. None of us had. I took a tiny measure of comfort from that.

Dr. C. had insured his business extremely well, so none of us lost our jobs in the aftermath of the fire or during the long rebuilding process. In a remarkable stroke of luck, he was able to rent a vacant building almost directly across the street from the burned hospital, which would become our new workplace until the original facility was restored. Some remodeling work would also need to be done in the temporary location in order to convert it to a veterinary hospital, however, and in the meantime we found ourselves "homeless" with no place to see patients.

That didn't stop us, though. If our clients and patients couldn't come to us, we would simply go to *them*. And that's how for several months, we became a house call practice. Dr. D. and two techs would see appointments that way while Dr. C. and Tanya attended endless meetings with contractors, insurance agents, and the like. When a cat needed a treatment or procedure that we couldn't accomplish in the client's home- like X-rays or an anesthetic procedure- a deal was thrashed out with one or another veterinary hospital in town to borrow the use of their facilities. Another couple of staff members would spend the day at a storage unit which was pressed into service as a makeshift retail sales space for bags of prescription diets and other items our clients needed to buy. It made for a very different kind of working experience and took some getting used to, but we made it work, and most clients *and* their cats seemed to prefer the arrangement.

Alyssa's apartment and its contents hadn't been covered by Dr. C.'s business insurance, though he'd evidently led her to believe that it had been. He also still required her to pay the outstanding balance on her cats' account at the hospital- despite them all now being deceased. Hearing about this made it harder for me to continue trying to give Dr. C. the benefit of the doubt, as I'd been trying to do since seeing the strain on his face in the first few weeks immediately following the fire. But if it was hard for me, it had to be infinitely harder for Alyssa and her husband, and this seemed to effectively be the last straw for them where Dr. C. was concerned. Alyssa's departure from the hospital was still a little further down the line, but it had apparently been a long time coming even before the fire, which finally gave her the push she needed in order to leave the first job she'd ever had.

As for me, I was usually one of the techs assigned to be seeing patients with Dr. D. during this time period, and she and I ended up spending a lot of time in her car together as we shuttled from one appointment to another. We had *downtime* together for the first time, and opportunities to have conversations about things besides the immediate tasks right in front of us. I began to think of her as a real friend- something that had never happened with any other doctor I'd known- and I don't think I was alone in this. The unique circumstances of our work situation had largely dissolved the professional boundaries and formalities normally maintained between a DVM and support staff. The other techs and I might have still addressed her as "Doctor", but we increasingly thought of her as "one of us", and if her cheerful nature had been good for staff morale before- when things were *normal*- it now became a kind of glue helping to hold what remained of our team together.

I didn't see much of Dr. C. that fall and winter, not until he hosted the staff Xmas party at his home and announced that we would be moving into our temporary hospital space very soon. He gave each of us an expensive winter jacket embroidered with the hospital logo as a holiday gift, and made a little speech about "unity" and how the most important part of his practice couldn't be destroyed by the fire because it was *us* that made it what it was. It was a nice speech, and it might have even made me a little misty-eyed.

Michelle, however, was not impressed. She and I had ended up as "Secret Santa" to each other and naturally gravitated towards each other at the party. She dryly (and quietly) pointed out that the jackets which he'd said he intended as an expression of "unity" also essentially amounted to advertisements for his business which we were required to wear, and she would have preferred a bonus in her paycheck. She said she would bet that he just hadn't wanted us covering up the logo on our uniform shirts with our *own* coats this winter- not when we *could* be "walking billboards," as she put it.

I shrugged and admitted that I guessed that did sound more like the Dr. C. I had come to know, and I noticed that Michelle didn't put her jacket on as she stood preparing to leave the party, though the night was cold. She was on her way back to the hospital for evening kennel duties; the holiday season always packed the clinic *full* of boarding patients, and Dr. C. loved seeing every cage filled. Michelle and I, on the other hand, dreaded it because of the speed with which upper respiratory infections can spread through a kennel full of cats.

"At least it's not as bad this year as it's been other years," she said now. "There was one Thanksgiving when he wanted us to just keep packing them in even when we ran out of cages. We were boarding cats in their *carriers*."

"What? You mean, for their entire stay?" I couldn't imagine how cramped and uncomfortable those poor cats must have felt. But she nodded and said that of course the clients hadn't been told that.

"We hid them in the storage closet if somebody asked to look at the kennel," she added.

I couldn't believe I'd been feeling sympathetic towards Dr. C. just a few minutes before. But it was the holiday season at the end of a rough year, and I wanted to think peaceful thoughts. I wanted to believe the new year and the new workspace would bring more changes for the better. And so that's what I believed for a while.

CHAPTER SEVEN

It took a couple of months for us to settle into our new workspace, and for word to spread among our client base that we were back to our pre-fire service capabilities and appointment availability. Everyone had to adjust to the new floor plan, the new exam room layouts, and new ways of running the daily operations as mandated by the new space.

The new building had issues with leaks during heavy rain (a frequent occurrence in New Orleans, which once memorably resulted in Dr. D. and I finishing a spay surgery while standing in ankle-deep water pushed into the building by cars driving through the flooded street). It was located on "the wrong side" of that street, closer to the edge of a rough neighborhood that some of our clients were fearful of approaching. It was an awkward and challenging time for the whole team, a painfully slow-feeling crawl back to "normal" which seemed to worsen Dr. C.'s characteristic impatience, and we lost a few more staff members along the way.

Michelle didn't stay on much longer after the holiday party; in fact, she and Alyssa ended up making the same career switch, with both joining the staff of New Orleans' Audubon Zoo. Another tech switched paths entirely and opted to become an exotic dancer on Bourbon Street.

Once again- just like at my first job back in Atlanta- I found myself suddenly counted among the hospital's more senior staff members, and after being there for less than a year. Neither Alyssa nor Michelle was easy to replace, and Dr. D. and Dr. K. (who'd recently returned from maternity leave) both began to rely on me more as Tanya went through one new hire after another looking for a good fit.

I don't recall if I ever knew where else Tanya might have worked before, or what her previous experience as a hiring manager might have been. But it seemed to me that one big reason she was having so much trouble finding good candidates was that the only forum where she would advertise an open position was Craigslist, where she could do so at no cost whatsoever. In her place, I would have published ads in the classified listings of one or more of the veterinary industry publications that I knew Dr. C. subscribed to (because he left them lying all over the hospital). I would scan these ads- along with *everything* else in those magazines- whenever I had a rare opportunity to actually *sit down and eat lunch* at some point during the day. By now, I'd had to help train enough other veterinary support staff (at both jobs in both states) that I knew the kind of co-worker I wished Tanya would hire, and I knew that the way she was going about it wasn't the way to attract them.

I wanted co-workers who genuinely shared my passion for helping animals, as I'd once believed *all* veterinary personnel did. But five years of working behind the scenes in a variety of situations and locales had taught me that this quality can be rarer in veterinary medicine than the average pet caregiver wants to believe, and an unwillingness on the part of hospitals to invest in their support staff is often a root cause.

I couldn't say for sure whether Tanya's refusal to spend a single cent on quality, targeted advertising for a new tech was her own decision or a rule handed down by Dr. C., but most of the applicants she got from Craigslist were simply looking for any job they could get. Some meant well and tried to do their best, but simply couldn't master many of the required skills quickly enough, while others were there primarily to collect a paycheck, not to dedicate themselves to saving and improving cats' lives, and it showed in the way they went about their tasks. They were sloppy and inconsistent, and displayed an infuriating (at least to me) lack of understanding regarding the gravity of what they were doing when they were tasked with something like monitoring patients recovering from surgery or making sure an exam table was disinfected between appointments. I wouldn't have trusted them to take care of my own cats in my absence because I couldn't trust their unsupervised work, and it both amazed and frustrated me to no end that Tanya and Dr. C. *did* trust them. They never seemed to want to fire anyone who wasn't working out once they'd hired them; neither one ever wanted to admit they'd made a mistake, and this could be *dangerous* to patients. I worried that sooner or later, something would happen that would be far worse than when the dog had been left outdoors all night at my first job. It began to rankle me more and more when I heard either of them tell a client that "we treat your cats like they're our own". If they truly meant that, I thought, they would damn well be putting patient care *first,* instead of making it a lower priority than hiring as cheaply as possible and trying to get something for nothing with every job interview Tanya conducted.

This was the same problem we'd had back in Atlanta, when Roberta had been more interested in giving second chances to down-on-their-luck misfits (who could also be hired very cheaply) than she was in recruiting dedicated animal medical professionals who put the patients first every day. This was the same problem we'd had when Dr. G. took over and was more interested in surrounding himself with people who would accommodate, accept, or enable his highly questionable behavior than he was in ensuring patients' safety in the hospital. This was the same problem I would hear about- time and time again- whenever we *did* manage to find a new team member who "got it", who was focused on the patients and who'd had some prior experience at one or more other animal hospitals in town. Evidently, if these people- the ones I *would* choose to be on the team with me- could be believed, then most hiring managers in the veterinary community of a given area tended to approach staffing in more or less the same way, whether it was Atlanta or New Orleans.

The common thread was that the hospitals *always* wanted to hire as cheaply as they could (and as sparingly as they could, too, in most cases). And because neither Georgia nor Louisiana required the title "veterinary technician" to mean anything real in terms of formal training, licensing, or qualifications, they always got away with doing so. (Again- twenty years later, this state of affairs has not changed significantly; many states still offer no title protection for veterinary technicians or nurses, and so hospitals are still legally able to do this. I advise all pet caretakers to check your own state's requirements and ask questions at your vet clinic or hospital to find out whether they employ licensed, formally trained personnel to care for your beloved companions.)

It seemed to me that, despite any outward appearances to the contrary, most veterinary hospitals were essentially being staffed by skeleton crews of dedicated employees like Alyssa, Michelle, or myself, who cared about the patients and about the job being done right, and these people continually took up the slack for an endless string of others, inadvertently helping to mask the "revolving door" problem in their efforts to maintain a seamlessly acceptable standard of patient care. Not surprisingly, they'd eventually get burnt out, and try another hospital in hopes of finding better, like I often thought about doing, but hearing these stories confirmed for me that it made no sense for me to leave. I still loved working exclusively with cats, and hospitals where I could do that were still extremely limited in number. (New Orleans had one other feline hospital besides ours, and we'd already acquired two techs who had "defected" from that facility to ours in recent months with tales of a toxic workplace *there* as well.)

At some point in 2003 I came to accept that this was just the way things were in the veterinary field; these were just the facts of life that came with the job- at least in the southeast part of the country, it seemed. I had the sense- from skimming all those industry publications- that more generally progressive states like California or New York might still be better, but I might as well contemplate relocating to the moon, they both seemed so far away (and not just in geographical terms). I had long since given up on any plans I'd had to pursue journalism or creative writing in any serious way; despite the many stresses and frustrations of my job, it still gave me a deep sense of purpose and fulfillment that I knew I would never be able to find on a career path that did not involve helping animals in some capacity. My own two cats- my babies Merlin and Malachai- were gradually becoming mature adults who were beginning to collect a few more medical issues between them, and the employee discount at their doctor's office functioned as my fur-kids' health insurance- something *else* I knew I'd never find at any other kind of job.

And I admit that part of me liked being the one (or one of the few, depending on the turn of the revolving door) that Dr. D. and Dr. K. knew they could always depend on throughout the day to function as true *support* for their own tasks of diagnosing and forming treatment plans for patients. I felt valued and needed by them, if not so much by Tanya or Dr. C. (both of whom really seemed to believe that just about any warm body would do for the job).

The associate doctors always backed me up on the occasions when I tried to bring Tanya's attention to issues with new trainees (with her response usually being that the staff needed to work out interpersonal or training issues themselves). The problem was that neither Dr. D. or Dr. K. had any real say in hospital policies, administration, or the hiring or firing processes, but were forced to essentially just soldier on like the dedicated skeleton crew members that they were, often having to do many things themselves that doctors should be able to entrust to their nurses unquestioningly.

Dr. K. was particularly appreciative of techs she could rely on because there had been many tasks she'd been completely unable to do during her recent pregnancy (although cleaning litterpans, incidentally, had *not* been one of those things. She was the first person to explain to me that the advice doctors commonly give to pregnant women- about avoiding contact with cats or litterboxes due to the risk of toxoplasmosis- is an overabundance of caution, and that rubber gloves and/or a thorough handwashing after cleaning a litterbox will amply suffice to avoid any such risk. This is true even in cases of cats *known* to be shedding the parasite, which is furthermore rare in cats who do not consume wild prey or other raw meat29).

Once I'd realized that I was most likely going to be a "lifer" in the veterinary field despite its difficulties and shortcomings, I found I wanted to learn as much as I possibly could as a support staff member about every aspect of the profession- the business side as well as the medical side. I took an interest in looking for ways to help our hospital become the best it could possibly be. I started reading *Veterinary Practice News, DVM360,* and the others more avidly, sometimes even taking them home with me because there was seldom time to finish reading even a short article during the workday. Dr. C. never missed them before I brought them back, and I wondered if he ever actually read them himself.

I can remember suggesting things in staff meetings for our team to try based on something I'd read about "streamlining the workflow for maximum efficiency", for example, or things for us to offer our clients that no other veterinary hospitals in town were offering, like kitten socialization classes (aka "Kitten Kindergarten" classes). Similar to puppy-training classes for newer or less experienced cat parents, these classes are becoming more common in the United States nowadays, but they were a brand-new idea in the U.S. veterinary market in the early 2000s, imported from Australia30. I'd been quite excited to read about them, immediately seeing their potential usefulness in reducing the demand for declaw surgeries, which was something else I was determined to accomplish at our hospital.

My suggestions were usually met with polite thanks and belabored explanations as to why they weren't practical or "wouldn't work with our clients". I was becoming *that* staff member who always has something else to bring up during the meeting, when everyone else is more than ready to go home. I'm not sure why I thought Tanya or Dr. C. would listen to me about any of these other things when they wouldn't listen to me about new staff members not working out, but I persisted for a while.

I can't recall any of my ideas ever being implemented (or even given a try), but in the fall of 2003 Dr. C. astonished me by selecting me to attend that year's convention of the American Association of Feline Practitioners (AAFP) along with him and Dr. K. It was my understanding that it had been his habit for the past several years to bring one of the techs along whenever he attended any big veterinary conferences being held in town; he'd previously taken Alyssa with him more than once, but even in her absence, I'd never expected to be his next choice.

He and I still tended to regard each other with a mutual attitude of resigned tolerance, and got along best when we were around each other the least- at any rate, that's how it always felt to me. I thought that one of our more recent hires- a girl I'll call "Marnie"- would be in line for this honor sooner than me, since she seemed to get along well with Dr. C. and was already looking like a candidate to move into Alyssa's old apartment above the hospital when the original building was restored. (It was driving Dr. C. *crazy* that we were still unable to offer 24-hour care on the premises as we'd done before the fire, and he was hounding the construction workers across the street on a daily basis to complete the work faster. But I never heard him talk about how much better it would be for our hospitalized patients. I only ever heard him complain about how the continued inability to provide it was making him "hemorrhage money".)

Maybe he'd invited Marnie to the convention first and she hadn't wanted to go, or perhaps Dr. K. or Dr. D. had persuaded him to offer it to me instead; I can't recall if I ever knew for sure. I liked Marnie and considered her one of Tanya's hiring successes, but I wouldn't have expected her to want to attend a veterinary conference on her own time; although good at the job, she didn't strike me as a "lifer" the way Alyssa had, or the way I considered myself to be. While I didn't

necessarily relish the idea of spending time with Dr. C. outside of the
hospital and my regular work duties, I did consider it an honor to be
chosen, and a fantastic educational opportunity- like reading a whole
stack of industry publications in a single weekend. And Dr. K. would
be there too, after all, and would be an excellent buffer between us, I
reasoned. So I was in.

I remember getting to sit in on mini-seminars and panel
discussions about anesthesia, pain management, and the importance
of observing the whole patient in the veterinary intensive care unit
and not merely their vital signs ("ICU should mean *I see you*", I can
still hear one panelist saying emphatically). I remember poring over
the books for sale in the vendors' area for what seemed like hours-
real veterinary medical textbooks and journals that I'd never (especially
at that time) have had the opportunity to purchase anywhere else or
under any other circumstances. There were probably dozens I wanted,
but they were pricy for any vet tech's salary; these books were meant
for people with advanced medical degrees and the salaries that went
with them. I settled for just the most affordable one of them, which still
sits on my bookshelf today- *Feline Behavior: A Guide For Veterinarians,
Second Edition* by Bonnie V. Beaver, DVM, MS, Dipl. ACVB.

And I remember having lunch with Dr. K. and Dr. C. at the House
of Blues in the French Quarter during a break in the conference
programming. At one point Dr. C. left the table to take a phone call
and Dr. K. said she was glad that he'd brought me because she knew
I would get a lot out of being at the conference, whereas in the past
he'd tended to take "people who would be impressed" by his status as a
requested speaker at these events.

That still didn't give me much insight into why he'd picked *me* this
time (did he really think I would be similarly impressed by something
like that?), but I didn't care. I *was* getting a lot out of being there,
and I had plans to use it all to improve our patients' experiences in
the hospital as well as their lives at home. (I think Dr. C. may have

later come to regret bringing me along when I started clamoring in staff meetings for things like a pulse oximeter in the surgery suite or a laryngoscope to make intubation go more smoothly. He hadn't counted on me learning how to pinpoint and spotlight the ways in which our daily operations were falling short of the gold standard, despite our reputation to the contrary.)

Being at the conference now was also giving me the idea to become licensed as a real veterinary technician. For a while, the more I'd been reading and learning, the more I had begun to realize there was that I *didn't* know about how to do my job. It disturbed me that I wouldn't know how to stabilize a crashing patient without a doctor there telling me exactly what to do and when to do it, and most of us were the same way, to one extent or another. I didn't think that should be acceptable for "nurses" who administered anesthetic drugs, assisted with surgeries, and were often left to monitor anesthetized patients alone for many minutes while the doctor was pulled away to handle something else.

If we were nurses, I thought it wasn't unreasonable to expect that we should all know *how to save lives* in an emergency, but I wasn't confident that any of us did. I suppose I had a form of imposter syndrome, but I didn't know that phrase at the time. I just knew that I would feel much more confident and capable at work if I felt like I'd had enough in-depth medical training, but even after years of working in veterinary settings, I still only knew what the doctors felt I *needed* to know... and as long as there was a DVM there, what techs "needed" to know wasn't considered to be all that much. (Once again, pet parents: if it's important to you for your animal's *entire* vet staff to be well educated and trained, check your state's legal requirements for this, and if your vet isn't required to hire licensed professionals, let them know you'd still like to see it.)

I guess it was due to the excitement of being at the conference, of suddenly feeling so immersed in everything I'd been trying to learn more about, of feeling closer than I'd ever been before to my childhood dream of "doing" veterinary medicine... that I impulsively confided in Dr. K. about this new idea of mine. I naively thought that if Tanya and Dr. C. didn't want to hire a licensed tech because they would have to pay them more, they would still surely look favorably on one they'd already hired being willing to *become* licensed. Employers always wanted workers who took the initiative, who wanted to learn more and better themselves... right?

Dr. K. tried to let me down gently. "Well... you'd probably have to pay for the program yourself," she said with a slightly pained expression. "They *might* be willing to work around your class schedule, but you'd lose hours for sure. And you know they wouldn't be required to give you a pay raise or anything, don't you?" I said that wasn't why I wanted to do it, and she replied that in that case, it really wouldn't benefit me to do it, because most veterinary employers in the state would be the same way. "They can't teach people how to care, and you already know how to do that. We can teach you the rest," she said.

"Um... yeah, I suppose so," I replied, crestfallen. But I thought to myself: *Yeah, right. There's never any time for that.* I knew how much faster and easier it is to do something yourself than to teach someone else how to do it.

"And besides..." she added, seeing my face. "What would I do without you there?" She patted my arm consolingly. "You know we always need all hands on deck."

Oh, I knew *that,* all right. And so I let go of the idea. I told myself that better skills and more confidence would come with more time on the job, through sheer osmosis if need be, and that simply being there to help was the most important thing I could do.

I was beginning to get very good at telling myself that things were OK when they weren't.

Declawing cats was definitely not OK. It hadn't taken long for me to realize this after beginning to see more of it on the job in New Orleans than I had back in Atlanta. Not only was the procedure more in demand among Dr. C.'s clients than it had been with the client base Dr. G. had inherited from Dr. F., but I couldn't escape from the surgery suite to the front desk anymore, as it had been so easy for me to do back then. Now I saw it all; even on days when I wasn't the surgical tech, I would typically be involved in some aspect of the aftercare, since declaw patients typically stayed in the hospital anywhere from 24- 72 hours.

I saw some smooth recoveries and some very, very rough ones. I saw cats emerge from anesthesia peacefully, and I saw them wake up screaming and thrashing in agony, chewing their bandages off and painting the interiors of their cages with blood, which caused us to have to put them right back under sedation to get the hemorrhaging under control. Sometimes this wouldn't happen right away when they first woke up, but during the overnight hours, when no staff were on the premises and patients were left completely unattended. I sometimes had nightmares about being the first one to arrive at work the morning after a declaw surgery, finding a cat bleeding out, and having to deal with it alone.

Some cats reportedly did well at home following the surgery (according to their caretakers), but others returned with infected paws, visibly limped, had trouble jumping or climbing, or seemed afraid to step in the litterbox and sought out soft items like clothes or bedsheets for eliminating. Infections of varying severity were probably the most common occurrence. It's virtually impossible to keep freshly declawed paws clean for the entire healing process unless the cat remains hospitalized the entire time (or on cage rest at home), and few clients were willing to pay those kinds of bills or do that degree of nursing work themselves. Some cats became withdrawn and depressed, or showed other behavioral changes ranging from "being less affectionate" to "hating everybody now". (This was vividly illustrated for me by one patient in particular, a Himalayan kitten named Dexter who the techs had referred to as "the living cotton ball" due to how easy he'd been to handle prior to being declawed, and who'd morphed into a screaming, biting bundle of PTSD at every visit afterward.)

I've never tried to claim that *every* onychectomy is an unmitigated horror story, the way the U.S. veterinary establishment has portrayed "animal rights activists" as doing when the former has been actively lobbying against legislation aiming to ban the procedure. But a lot of them *were* horrific.

It didn't seem to matter which doctor did the surgery or which method they used (Dr. C. of course favored the old-school Resco guillotine method, the fastest and cheapest way of doing it, while Dr. D. used the cleaner and more precise scalpel disarticulation method which demanded more patience and care, but it didn't guarantee her surgical patients a better outcome). We didn't have a surgical laser, which surprises me in hindsight because Dr. C. was always extremely keen on offering his clients the most technologically advanced and cutting-edge services he could; not only did he love using fancy gadgets himself, but they added so much *perceived value* for clients, they'd be willing to pay higher exam fees!

In the case of a surgical laser, I can only guess that he must have run the numbers and decided that it would be too difficult- given his clients' ability at the time to *perceive the value* of laser surgery- for him to recoup the cost of the equipment plus the profit he'd require to make it worth his while. But I still wouldn't have felt good about declawing cats even had we had a laser; to me declawing was ethically questionable at best regardless of the method, and I was far from being an "animal rights activist"- at the time I still ate meat, wore leather, and (don't forget!) had once even thought I would want a declawed cat *myself.* But I knew now that even when done by the best surgeons available, and even when using "better" methods, declawing still subjects the patient to *intense* pain and stress, as well as the risks associated with general anesthesia (for a medically unnecessary procedure), and it still alters their body, abilities, biomechanical functioning, and life forever.

I thought now that if I were a cat, I would probably be hard-pressed to find a meaningfully significant difference in my pain or difficulty if my toes were cut off by a laser beam instead of a scalpel blade, and indeed: in 2014, a Canadian study comparing the three methods of declawing concluded that while laser onychectomy was associated with a reduced rate of short-term postoperative complications such as bleeding and infection, "there was no detectable difference in the long-term outcome of cats regardless of the method used"[31.]

Our hospital was objectively one of the best medical facilities for cats in the country at that time, with Dr. C.'s board certification in feline medicine being even rarer than it still is today. But despite his advanced degrees and technical expertise, and despite all the tender loving care that both Dr. D. and Dr. K. brought to the table, we still had a higher rate of surgical complications and suboptimal results with declaw procedures than we did with any other surgery, as far as I could tell. Any other elective procedure with such a high risk of an adverse outcome would probably be dropped from our services, but not so with declawing.

It *obviously* caused harm to cats, and I don't think any of us were in denial about that basic fact. But all three doctors were convinced that we provided ample pain management (even when it often was very clearly not enough- those cases were *anomalies,* they insisted).

Individually, Dr. C. believed that declawing was every cat owner's right; Dr. D. professed to hate it but to have "made her peace" with doing it because "it means they'll get to stay in a good home," and- still only working part-time with a newborn at home- Dr. K. usually didn't do surgeries at all. The motto of most of the other techs- at least as far as they would discuss at work- seemed to be "the doctors said it, I believe it, and that settles it!" or words to that effect. The receptionists never had to take care of (or even really *see)* the cats in pain "in the back". So the only one out of the entire staff who was facing a crisis of conscience about taking part in declawing cats, it seemed, was me.

Declawing a cat in a veterinary hospital makes a mockery and hypocrisy of everything else that's done there "to prevent and relieve animal suffering". There was no way around this for me, nothing I could tell myself that made it feel any different at the end of the day. For a while I took Dr. D.'s words at face value when she'd say things like: "If we didn't declaw these cats, their people would just take them somewhere else to have it done, and another hospital won't do as good a job as we will."

I knew that we used a much more comprehensive multimodal pain management protocol than most other hospitals would (it included using lidocaine to block the nerves in the cats' paws, and applying a fentanyl transdermal patch to the back of their neck after the surgery), so Dr. D.'s reasoning did make a measure of sense for a short time. But the sheer amount (and *strength*) of pain medication that was required to mitigate the damage we were doing was a constant red flag to me that it just wasn't right. (And that was years before I connected with other veterinary support staff on social media and learned that evidently, virtually every DVM who declaws cats has told their staff some variation of this line- the implication being that they *all* seem to believe they're the best in their area at what they do. Or are they merely trying to keep their dissenting staff members in line?)

I tried talking to clients in appointments when they asked about declawing their cats, explaining that it was very hard on them and there are lots of training techniques and tips for protecting furniture so that they wouldn't need to resort to surgery. I was told by Tanya in no uncertain terms that it was the doctor's job to discuss with clients whether surgery was indicated, not mine (and I couldn't help thinking of the former employees she'd told me about in my interview- the ones who'd disagreed with the doctors about spaying pregnant cats.

I'd actually assisted with a pregnant spay by this time, though, and although it did make me sad, I'd been confident the kittens had no awareness of what was happening, and I didn't believe the two procedures were comparable in terms of ethical considerations. Declawing often resulted in a great deal more pain and suffering, and it lacked mitigating factors such as reducing pet overpopulation or protecting the patient from reproductive cancers).

So then I tried bringing Dr. D. the articles I was reading about kitten kindergarten classes, or I'd photocopy chapters for her from *Feline Behavior: A Guide For Veterinarians (Second Edition)*. While it bothered me that the book endorsed declawing as a "lifesaving" surgery for cats facing euthanasia due to behavioral problems, I thought (at the time) that this was well tempered by detailed discussions of the reasons and motives for natural feline behaviors, and how to teach clients to successfully modify or redirect their cats' scratching. Most importantly, it was written in the peer-reviewed language of doctors and scientists, so I figured doctors should be able to take it seriously. Dr. D. always seemed interested, saying that she'd love to read whatever I'd brought her, and she hoped she would find the time... "soon". I tried everything I could think of to work within the system of our small hospital to effect change, and I tried to keep the faith in the meantime.

I tried to take inspiration from the autistic academician and animal behaviorist Temple Grandin, who wrote about her work within the agricultural industry to build a less terrifying slaughterhouse for the cows she loved because she knew she'd never be able to stop people from eating meat in her lifetime. Maybe I'd try starting a little more modestly and seeing if I could at least talk the doctors out of doing any more *full* declaw surgeries on all four paws (something that was beginning to fall out of favor with other vets even back then). Here again, our doctors believed that if *any* hospital should be performing these still-requested surgeries, *ours* should because we were "the best".

But I thought I could work on persuading Dr. D., and she would hopefully then work on convincing Dr. C.

And then there was Ralph.

The local SPCA facility at that time was located in New Orleans' 9th ward, another neighborhood which many people avoided- well, people like our clients, at any rate. It was believed by our doctors (and apparently the SPCA staff as well) that genteel, well-to-do New Orleanians wanting to adopt new pets were often put off by the surroundings at the shelter, and efforts were made to showcase animals in other locations as often as possible. To that end, our hospital had a partnership with the SPCA wherein we were usually housing an adoptable cat or two for them at any given time so that our clients could see them, visit with them, and perhaps take one home. This in turn would also empty a cage at the SPCA so another cat could be housed there. Dr. C. liked doing this because it often gained him new patients- and it made him look like he was giving back to the community at the same time (appearances were very important to him).

Ralph was an SPCA cat of whom I'd grown particularly fond. He was remarkably easygoing and friendly for a cat who'd been "eartipped" at some point in his life, marking him as feral. He seemed to bond easily with just about any human who cared for him, and he was a favorite among most of the staff, not just me. I don't recall exactly how long he was with us, but it was ridiculously long for any cat with such a sweet and affable personality to go without finding a home. Several other cats had come and gone in the time we'd had him. Possibly the eartip and the fact that he was obviously not a kitten anymore were working against him.

I wished heartily that I could adopt him myself, but my husband and I were at our limit with two; even with a substantial employee discount, their healthcare costs added up quickly at our hospital. On top of that, our boys already had an ongoing turf war in our apartment, competing fiercely for the most prized sleeping spots as well as our attention, and I knew adding a third cat would strain their relationship even further and be unfair to both of them (yes, there *is* such a thing as having too many cats for the space and resources one can provide, despite what a million Internet memes may say!)

So I contented myself with taking care of Ralph at work, spoiling him now and then with treats, catnip, or extra "walkabout" time when I could, and being glad that at least with us, he would be safe from ending up on the list to be euthanized at the shelter for lack of space.

When a client finally showed a serious interest in adopting Ralph, initially I was happy for him and was keeping my fingers crossed. The SPCA had final approval of all the adoption applications, but established clients of our hospital were essentially shoo-ins, so it really just came down to the client making up her mind. I lingered in the hallway behind the reception area, sweeping a spot that was already clean and trying to eavesdrop as she chatted with Tanya after visiting Ralph. I didn't know this client; she must have been relatively new to our hospital, but she'd seemed nice. It sounded like she was asking Tanya for details about how to submit the adoption application.

And then I heard Tanya say: "Don't tell them that you want to declaw, or else they won't adopt to

you."

I was shocked. Even if my clamoring for our hospital to stop declawing cats was falling on deaf ears, even if I was the only one there who felt strongly that it was wrong, I still would never have imagined that anyone there would have advised a client to try to deceive the SPCA about their intentions in such a manner, particularly since the adoption agreement (with its clause prohibiting declawing) was technically a legally binding contract. But whether this was something they told people all the time or whether Tanya just thought we'd kept Ralph for long enough, I'd heard what I'd heard.

It felt like the last straw for me. In that moment, I could no longer convince myself that I was in a good place, doing good things. I was utterly disgusted. I thought of sweet, lovable Ralph on the surgery table having his toes amputated for no good reason, and I had to go and hide in the restroom and cry silently. It didn't end up happening, as I would later hear; Ralph and the woman's resident cat got along well enough that she changed her mind about it. But for me, the damage had been done; I thought I would never be able to muster quite the same degree of faith in my profession again. If this was the kind of thing a veterinary hospital could do and still be considered among the best of the best, I thought dismally- then what must things be like at the *rest*? By the early summer of 2004, I'd submitted my two weeks' notice.

CHAPTER EIGHT

A while before I left the feline hospital, my husband had *joined* the staff there, moving over from the nearby boarding and grooming facility where he'd been working since before the fire, so at least our kids didn't lose their specialized (and discounted!) healthcare when I finally quit. We hadn't planned things that way, but I was relieved and glad my children could still be seen and treated by Dr. D., and that we'd still be able to afford it. (I needn't really have worried; Dr. C. never turned away any cat whose humans were willing to pay him, and providing services for staff pets at a discount was still better than losing those patients and that revenue altogether.)

I tried to get a completely different kind of job after leaving; I felt burnt out on veterinary medicine by this point and wanted to do just about anything else. Outside of veterinary work, my most marketable skills were of the office/clerical variety, but I hadn't updated them in a few years- well, almost *ten* years in fact had passed since I had really beefed up or polished my resume, I realized. The world had changed. The only business or office software I was familiar with were veterinary practice management programs.

I remember trying a temp service and getting discouraged very quickly; I can also recall trying for numerous positions offered by the human resources department at Tulane University. I even considered applying to Tulane as a *student* in the law school, but in a meeting with financial aid advisors, I was told that I'd need to practice some lucrative form of corporate law for several years before being able to do the environmental protection work I was interested in, just to be able to pay off my student loans. This effectively soured me on the idea. (And this is how I learned that the high cost of higher education can often result in a paucity of ethical principles among the very professionals- our doctors and lawyers- in whom we wish to see the *highest* ethical standards.)

Nothing was happening quickly enough, and our checking account balance was dipping lower and lower. So when I heard that another animal hospital in town needed a receptionist, I didn't feel that I had much choice but to apply there. I convinced myself that going back to working at a front desk rather than being hands-on with the patients would be much better for me- much less stressful- and that since it would be another mixed practice, most of the patients would probably be dogs, and I wouldn't have to feel like I was their only strong advocate at the hospital. *Everybody* in the veterinary world was always looking out for dogs, or so it seemed.

And so, in the summer of 2004 I started working for Dr. Z. in another part of town. His practice felt very much like a family, largely because his daughter was about to graduate from vet school herself and had already partially joined the staff at her father's small hospital, which was planned to become hers when he was ready to retire. The office manager and her younger sister (who served as another receptionist) were the daughters of a close friend of Dr. Z., and they'd grown up thinking of him like an uncle. A third receptionist- "Gwen", the one I'd been hired to replace since she lived in New Orleans for only part of each year- was another longtime friend of Dr. Z. who exuded a grandmotherly vibe.

The only problem with this practice feeling so much like a family was that it could be very hard for new employees to fit into such a close-knit core group and find their footing. I gathered right away from Gwen that this hospital had its fair share of staff turnover too, and that Dr. Z. probably didn't expect me to be working there for very long. It sounded as if he'd become resigned to losing staff members, and so he tended to depend on just a few- which sounded familiar. Usually, it was just hoped that anybody he'd hurriedly hired to fill in for Gwen would last until she returned from New Mexico, where she and her husband went at the start of hurricane season each year to avoid the stress of "living in the cone of error", as she put it. She was due to leave again

soon, and had been reminding Dr. Z. he needed to find a temporary
replacement before she went.

So: Here was another veterinary hospital owner who seemingly
put little time or thought into finding the best and most qualified
candidates to fill his support staff positions, apparently because he
viewed it as wasted effort. *Whatever,* I thought. *Same problem, different
reason.* I was used to this by now, and I'd learned my lesson about
thinking I could change anything about the way vets chose to run their
hospitals.

I'd been as honest as I felt I could about the reason I'd left the feline
hospital without appearing to disparage it, and now I just wanted to
keep my head down, do my job as well as I could, and go home and
forget about it until the next morning. I hoped I *wouldn't* still be there
by the time Gwen returned to take back her position; for months I
continued trying to find another job (when I had the energy) on my
days off. But as the Great Revolving Door of veterinary support staff
kept revolving and I began to last longer than the average new hire
once *again,* I gradually found myself working more and more hours,
and settling into the job more. The two sisters who thought of Dr. Z.
like an uncle began to warm up to me, after being initially quite cold
and then seemingly deciding I'd proven myself in some unspoken way.
Eventually, I started rediscovering an emotional resilience I thought I'd
lost; a renewed ability to look on the bright side, to accept the things I
couldn't change and to change the things I could.

When Dr. Z. realized I was a more responsible and competent
worker than he'd hoped for, he was quick to give me more
responsibility, and even *better* from my perspective, he seemed more
and more willing to listen to my opinions about how the techs should
try to handle a frightened cat in an appointment, or why declawing was
a procedure that needed to fall by the wayside.

Despite being an older vet with a more old-fashioned way of doing
things than I'd become accustomed to, he had a kindly nature, and

he agreed that declawing could be traumatic for the patient and often failed to have the desired effect on behavior. He said that he still felt he should continue to offer it as an option for his clients, however. His practice was in a more socioeconomically disadvantaged neighborhood than where the feline hospital was located, and he said he'd seen too many clients bring in dogs with mangled ears or tails- which they'd attempted to crop at home themselves- not to think that some people would try to declaw their cats at home themselves, as well. The idea of that horrified me, but for comparison, this was a city and state where *cockfighting* was still legal at the time; the Louisiana SPCA wouldn't successfully lobby to have it banned until 2008[32]. Animal cruelty was a not-uncommon reality in the city, stemming sometimes from malice, sometimes from ignorance, and sometimes from both.

I didn't doubt or dismiss what Dr. Z. was saying, but I countered that it was still a better goal for us to teach such clients why they *shouldn't* declaw their cat than it was for us to simply accommodate them because we were assuming the worst about what they'd do if we didn't.

Dr. Z. admitted that was food for thought, and I counted this as a victory. Our periodic debates continued; on another occasion, I pointed out to Dr. Z. that when clients asked him about cropping their dogs' ears or tails, he typically told them he didn't like to do it and gave them his reasons why, but he never tried very hard to talk his cat-owning clients out of declawing, so there was a double standard. His response was that he believed a client who couldn't crop their dog's ears or tail would probably still keep the dog, but a client denied access to declawing would be more likely to dump their cat in a shelter or simply throw them out the door.

"But my point is, you *talk to the client about it* when it's about a dog," I said. "They might not dump their cat if you talk to them about why you don't like to declaw."

And so we'd go round and round, and for a while there was a running joke between us (except I wasn't joking) that if I would agree to give up my precious and much-sought-after Saturdays off to help the clinic run more smoothly on its busiest day, Dr. Z. would then stop declawing. He always claimed to be considering it. But I had been right about feline patients and declawing being a relatively small part of what we did there in contrast to my last job, and now the mere fact that Dr. Z. was at least willing to listen to my concerns made a big difference in how I felt about going to work every day. I would never be okay with declawing, but maybe I could learn to make my own peace with it, the way Dr. D. and so many other veterinary professionals had done (and still do today). I *had* to make my peace with it; I simply felt I had no other real choice. I needed a job, and veterinary jobs were seemingly the easiest to come by, at least thus far.

I'd been there for about a year when a cat named Grendel was brought in to be declawed one day along with her housemate Beowulf. There was nothing about them or their medical histories that hinted at the vastly different outcomes the two cats would have. I don't recall anything that stood out about their cases until the clients returned to the hospital with Grendel a few days after both cats had been discharged following their surgeries. She'd been limping and holding up one front paw at home, seemingly unable to put her weight on it. Beowulf appeared to be recovering well and was behaving normally, the clients reported, but Grendel was refusing food and hissing at them whenever they got near her.

It turned out Grendel had a raging infection in one of her healing toe stumps, for which Dr. Z. put her on a strong antibiotic. The infection was lanced and drained, and the entire hospital could hear Grendel screaming while this was done. The clients were sent home with instructions to try to keep the paw clean- especially after Grendel used the litterbox- and to return for a recheck after finishing the antibiotics. She really should have been kept in the hospital with experienced techs doing this, but of course the clients hadn't budgeted for that. So Dr. Z. urged them to call us if they didn't start seeing an improvement in her appetite or behavior once getting the antibiotics on board.

They called a few days later, saying Grendel seemed worse instead of better, and when Dr. Z. reexamined her and took an X ray, it was determined that the infection was spreading up the bones of her paw and into her bloodstream, and was now threatening her life. The entire paw was going to need to be amputated, and as soon as possible. When the clients hesitated, Dr. Z. offered to do it at a substantial discount because he felt badly about the whole thing.

Poor Grendel. The clients authorized the additional surgery- to most of the staff's surprise after they'd declined to pay for hospitalization- but it was clear that the experience of trying to medicate her and treat her paw at home had been quickly eroding whatever degree of the human-animal bond had existed between them in the first place; the husband and wife had both been bitten, and were now saying that amputating her paw "better fix her".

She came through the second surgery all right, and as far as I was able to gather from the doctors and techs, was doing reasonably well in the hospital afterward. But then, we were forced to discharge her too early once again, and no one was very surprised when she continued exhibiting "aggressive" behavior at home and continued difficulties recovering. She finally lost her life when the clients decided enough was enough, and they told Dr. Z. to euthanize her.

I don't even recall the reason they'd given for wanting both cats declawed in the first place. But I remember Dr. Z. kind of hanging his head a little as he and I were closing the hospital that evening after the clients had left. I could tell he felt genuine regret about the way Grendel's case had gone. For my own part, I think I was just feeling numb with horror.

"You know... I'm starting to think that maybe you're right about declawing, after all," he said to me. That was music to my ears. I remember it all the more clearly because it was the last conversation about declawing (or any other matter relating to business-as-normal) that I was ever able to have with Dr. Z.

It was very shortly after this incident that Hurricane Katrina struck.

CHAPTER NINE

My husband and I didn't own a functional vehicle in the summer of 2005. We typically didn't really need one; a combination of walking, bicycling, and public transportation could get us virtually anywhere in the city we needed to go, and automobile maintenance and insurance were expensive. So when it became clear that the New Orleans metro area was under a serious threat from the massive storm that had just crossed the Florida peninsula and entered the Gulf, we were the only people we knew who were unable to evacuate, and no one offered to take us with them.

The prospect of staying in town was scary, but we had been through a few hurricane watches by now, and *nobody* expected this storm to be as devastating as it turned out to be. (Of course, the storm itself was never the real problem; it was later determined to be faulty construction work on the levees by the Army Corps of Engineers which resulted in the apocalyptic scene that unfolded after the storm had passed.)

Since we were going to be in town, it was assumed by Tanya and Dr. C. that my husband would take the weekend kennel duties at the cat hospital, which had always been shared between all the techs and kennel staff on a rotating basis, even back when Alyssa had been living upstairs. Dr. C. told my husband that we would both be welcome to stay in the hospital for the duration of the storm if need be; the restored building was assumed to be sturdier than our apartment building, and it had a second floor we could retreat to in the event of major flooding. In fact, it had a *third* floor, since Alyssa's (and later Marnie's) old living space was currently vacant again. So my husband and cats and I moved in as the weather began to deteriorate.

No real emergency plan had been put in place for the few cats staying in the hospital. There was a handful of boarders whose people hadn't been able to retrieve them for one reason or another, and a litter of kittens from the SPCA (I can't recall why *they* were not retrieved; possibly they were simply overlooked in the flurry of activity when the shelter put their own hurricane plan into effect).

I remember feeling very thankful that there weren't any seriously ill, hospitalized cats undergoing treatment at the time; I really don't know what we would have done if there had been. I didn't believe Dr. C. was allowing us both to stay there out of the goodness of his heart; he essentially also wanted us to act as his own private security force for his building and business, and at the bargain rate of just *one* kennel attendant's salary. Having us there was his way of covering his ass, I thought- but I didn't care. I did think my family would be safer in that building than in our home, and in an emergency, we'd have access to all kinds of lifesaving medications and equipment, even if our knowledge of how to use them was limited in the absence of a DVM.

While nobody expected Katrina to have the devastating impact that it did, there was really no excuse for the hospital to be as unprepared as they were for hurricane events, which have always been a basic fact of life in New Orleans. In contrast, Dr. Z.'s plan at his own hospital hadn't been perfect, but at least he'd *had* one; any animals left in the clinic were to be taken along with staff members to wherever they would be evacuating. And at my husband's former workplace- the boarding and grooming facility, which had since the fire been evolving into a nonprofit veterinary hospital and rescue/adoption agency- it turned out they had a lifeline in place to the vet school and ag center at LSU, which would later take in thousands of displaced and abandoned pets from all over the areas impacted by Katrina.

It was this nonprofit clinic that took our own two cats out of the city to safety after the storm, when news of the levee breach and the rapidly advancing floodwater was causing panic, looting, and chaos, and it was clear that my husband and I would not be able to hold off intruders determined to break into our hospital looking for drugs. When we saw the nonprofit clinic loading their animals into a transport van to shuttle them to LSU's animal hurricane shelter, we threw ourselves on their mercy and begged them to take our children with them, and I'll forever be grateful that they did.

I remember being on the phone with Dr. D. as we were preparing to leave, telling her what was going on and crying because we didn't know what to do about the rest of the cats we were trying to keep safe. A friend of ours who worked at the nonprofit clinic had promised to make sure our two boys would be taken to safety, but he didn't know how much room would be left in any of the vehicles quickly getting organized to leave from their facility, or how many more animals were still being brought together from the various other local rescue groups with which they were loosely affiliated. They would do what they could for our hospital's boarders, he said, but he couldn't promise more than he already had.

That didn't sound at all like a sure thing, so we needed a backup plan. I hadn't told Dr. D. that we'd already asked the nonprofit for help; their name was anathema to Dr. C. (and was supposed to be so to the rest of us by extension) due to longstanding tensions, rivalries, and philosophical differences between the two animal care facilities operating essentially on each other's doorsteps. Dr. D. told me that we should let all the cats out of their cages, open the windows of the hospital before we left, and trust the cats to do what they could to survive.

"Animals revert to nature in a disaster," she said. I couldn't imagine what might have been going through her mind when she said this, or whether she might have been easing her nerves with a bottle of wine, but my husband and I knew we could not do this in good conscience. If we had been the clients who were unable to get to the clinic to pick up our cats, the *last* thing we would have expected or wanted would be for our trusted vet's office to abandon them outdoors to fend for themselves, and I couldn't believe she'd actually told us to do that. To our great relief, the nonprofit clinic found enough space to fit all our boarders in among the animals they were already evacuating, and my husband and I made sure all their humans' contact information went with them. (They all made it back to their families safely, we later learned. But I don't like to imagine what might have happened to them had my husband and I been able to evacuate along with everyone else. Would some staff member have taken the boarding cats with them, the way the staff at Dr. Z.'s hospital was doing with their patients? Would anyone else have been willing to stay in town at the hospital, the way we'd been forced to do by our lack of options? We'll never know. My advice to pet parents- if the area in which you live is susceptible to hurricanes, tornadoes, floods, wildfires, earthquakes, or any other potentially catastrophic disaster- is to ask your vet clinic to explain their evacuation and emergency plans to you in detail. Don't simply assume that they will be prepared.)

With our own children and all the others safely on the road out of the nightmare the city was quickly falling into, my husband and I got ourselves out on our bicycles, pedaling over the (later infamous) Crescent City Connection just in time before it was locked down by police officers from a neighboring suburb wanting to prevent "any Superdomes over here"[33]. While looking for a pay phone at a gas station, we caught a ride with a truck driver heading to Baton Rouge, where there was a Red Cross shelter set up and where we would be closer to where we believed our cats had been taken.

We halfway expected Dr. C. to be angry about us enlisting the aid of the nonprofit clinic to save his patients; that was the depth of the mutual dislike that he and the woman who ran the other clinic had for one another, and I was sure he was going to hate the way it made him and his hospital look, both to his clients and his closest business rival. But he surprised us by expressing gratitude when we were finally able to get in touch with him.

I can't recall if we ever related to him the advice that Dr. D. had given us about releasing the cats; most likely that wasn't a priority in any conversation we had. It was a crazy and chaotic time, with the staff scattered all over several states and keeping in touch periodically and haphazardly by phone and e-mail. The same thing was going on with Dr. Z.'s staff- indeed, the same thing was going on with virtually everyone who had lived and worked in New Orleans just prior to August 29, 2005. My husband and I eventually ended up back in Georgia, a few hours' drive from Atlanta, when my brother-in-law came to collect us from the Red Cross shelter in Baton Rouge and put us up in his guest room instead.

It was clear that nobody's life was going to be getting back to normal anytime soon, but Dr. C. let us know that if we were able to return to New Orleans, we would have jobs. He was of course planning to reopen as soon as he possibly could, since he'd had minimal storm damage.

Dr. Z.'s hospital, it turned out, had flooded badly and it sounded like it would end up being declared a total loss. So it was good to know that I would be welcome to return to the feline hospital along with my husband, if I *wanted* to return. I was glad that I didn't have to make any decisions about anything right away; getting our own cats back with us was my first priority, and the only thing I was really able to think about.

To that end, we'd need to get a new apartment; *we* might have been welcome to stay at my brother-in-law's house for as long as we needed to, but our children were not. He'd pressured his wife to rehome her own cat when they married because he was vehemently opposed to animal hair or "those little rocks" (as he referred to cat litter) contaminating his home. So the logical thing for us to do, it seemed, was to relocate back to Atlanta for now, where things felt familiar and we still had some contacts.

Spurred on by my need to hold my babies again, we were settled in a tiny studio apartment in Atlanta- and on our way back to Louisiana in a rented car to pick them up from the hurricane shelter- within a fortnight. But it was three years before we were finally able to move back to New Orleans for what we thought would be for good.

CHAPTER TEN

Back in Atlanta, we found ourselves in dire need of new employment ASAP as our modest finances were strained by the costs of relocating and replacing most of our belongings. We also knew that if we decided to return to New Orleans, it would take time to save up the funds to do so. I was able to pick up a few shifts at my old retail job when someone called in sick, but not enough, and not consistently.

Predictably, the first interview I landed for full-time work was with another veterinary hospital. This was a large one with a huge client base spanning some of the more affluent neighborhoods of the city, and was known as "Atlanta's vet to generations of pets". The few hours I spent there in a working interview allowed me to see all I needed or wanted to know about what it would be like: everyone seemed stressed out and the environment felt chaotic and disorganized. I was familiar enough with toxic veterinary workplaces by now that I could recognize another one immediately, and I backed away from their job offer. No matter how badly I needed it, I just couldn't put myself through that particular kind of hell again right now. (In today's economic climate, I often hear on social media that "nobody wants to work", and I hear veterinary hiring managers in particular complaining that people will interview for jobs and then "ghost" the hospital, so perhaps I was ahead of the curve back in 2005. I have to wonder whether the problem today is really that "nobody wants to work" or whether some of these vanishing applicants might not be sensing something similar about their prospective work environment.)

Next I tried another veterinary hospital- another feline-exclusive clinic that I was excited and hopeful about because *they didn't declaw,* and they seemed to align with my standards and values in other ways as well. I was called back for a *second* working interview at this hospital, but the job offer this time finally went to someone else. My commute to work there on public transportation would be lengthy and convoluted, and despite my arrival at both working interviews on time with no issues, they evidently preferred their staff to have their own vehicles rather than being dependent on trains or buses- a common prejudice among Atlanta employers.

One day a neighbor and I struck up a conversation about the scrubs he was wearing, and it turned out that he worked at a nearby animal hospital and said he could probably get me a job there because they were short-staffed (*Surprise, surprise!* I thought). We were living not very far from our old neighborhood at the time, and I wondered if there were any new vet clinics that close by that I didn't know about. *It couldn't be,* I thought. *Could it?*

It could. My neighbor was working for Dr. G.

Of course, I had to explain at that point why I didn't think it would be a good idea for him to try getting me a job at the clinic. I didn't go into too many details; it would have been an awkward conversation to have. I said simply that Dr. G. had blamed me for missing drugs which I hadn't taken. The neighbor listened to my (highly abridged) story while shaking his head slowly in amazement.

"That's not the Dr. G. I know," he said. "That's not *my* Dr. G." I could only shrug. I was used to support staff members making excuses for the doctors they worked for by now, too.

When I ran into him on another occasion, he said that my story had bothered him so much he'd actually gone and talked to Dr. G. and Shelly about it, and had been told that "the whole thing was a big misunderstanding" caused by someone else who'd worked there at the time, and they were sorry it had happened. I couldn't help noticing that he didn't mention anything more about getting me a job at the clinic, but that was fine with me. Maybe Dr. G. had changed in the past few years, or maybe it was a case of his current employee wearing rose-colored glasses (I still suspect the latter), but in any case, I doubted he'd changed enough for our work styles to be compatible. The fact that this employee was actively trying to get people with veterinary experience to apply there told me that Dr. G. was still trying to do more business than his staff could handle well- like just about every vet I'd ever known after Dr.F.

And no matter *how* much he might have changed, there was no way I would ever be able to trust Dr. G. with my children's lives again. Not after what he'd done to Malachai, and the way he'd lied about it. I would never be able to forget or forgive *that*.

I took a telemarketing job for a few months and eventually went back to working in a movie theater in the spring of 2006. Like the retail job I'd had after parting ways with Dr. G., this felt like a step backward in some ways, but at the time it was what I wanted again. No matter how long or frustrating a shift might be at a job like that, I never had to worry about witnessing animals' sickness, trauma, or pain. Instead, all I had to worry about was whether there were enough tickets in the printer or enough ice at the soda fountain. There was literally *nothing* about the job that was so consequential as to merit getting stressed over. I could laugh at things that drove my (usually somewhat younger) co-workers crazy. One of the films that played at the theater while I worked there- *Clerks II*- summed up my feelings remarkably well on the poster hanging in the lobby: "With no power comes no responsibility." It certainly felt better than having no power and *all* the responsibility, the way it felt it had been for me in the veterinary world up to that point.

One evening as I waited on a long line of customers at the box office, I looked up from the ticket printer to see Marnie standing outside the window- Marnie from the cat clinic in New Orleans, who'd taken over for Alyssa for a while as the "night nurse" living in the apartment upstairs. We squealed upon recognizing each other and chatted for a minute or two while I counted her change for her tickets. She'd left the hospital prior to Katrina to pursue a more upscale career and lifestyle in Atlanta, and seemed stoked about it. I'd always suspected she wouldn't be a "lifer" in the veterinary world. It made me sad to realize that now, it didn't look like I would be, either. (I've since learned that I came closer to it than I believed I had at this point, however; it's been called "a commonly known fact" in the industry that the average lifespan for the career of a veterinary technician is a mere 5 to 7 years[34], so high is the rate of burnout.)

I even tried my hand at writing again. For most of 2007, I was working on a novel which I never finished, the provisional title of which was *Felinity*. I reasoned that I didn't necessarily need to be working in the veterinary field in order to help cats; my idea for the novel was to fill it with feline characters, give them human language, and do for them what Richard Adams' *Watership Down* had done for the public perception of rabbits in the 1970s. I thought that if I could get more humans to empathize deeply with cats, to understand them better, it would help to end the demand for declawing and lead to better treatment for them overall. It was the largest and most ambitious story I'd ever tried to write, and it suffered from a lack of focus. Worse, it suffered from my own nagging doubts that a fantasy story like the one I had in mind would be able to accomplish anything of the sort. But for a while it allowed me to feel like I was still doing something that at least had the *potential* to be important for cats.

We were fortunate that our own cats didn't need much medical care during this time, since we were more or less "between" doctors for them. There was one clinic we'd tried and were satisfied enough with, but I didn't "click" with any of the doctors there; none of them struck me as *cat* vets. (Ideally, I'd wanted the cat hospital where I'd been turned down for the job to be my new vet clinic. But while I still believed I could have made it to work there on time regularly using the bus and rail system, the distance and the difficulty of getting there with one or both of my kids in their carriers- especially in a medical emergency- made it too impractical to rely on them.)

My kids' issues of allergies and feline asthma were under control, and although both were mature adults, they weren't "old" or "senior" cats yet. (While the exact delineations between "adult", "senior", and "geriatric" can vary slightly, the consensus is that cats generally should not be thought of as elderly until they are *over* 10 years old[35], but the U.S. veterinary community and pet supply industry each have an overwhelming tendency to treat them as "seniors" beginning around age 7. While it's true that age-related changes can often be observed as young as 7 in cats, the use of this as a rubric is based on the lifespan of large dog breeds, in another example of the ways in which these industries have historically focused on and catered to dogs over cats and treated them as if they are the same. This is a potential problem for cats when their caretakers may decide not to pursue lifesaving treatments because they believe their pets' time is limited anyway. In reality, however, they may still have quite a few good years left.)

In December of 2007 my mother passed away, and we were forced to unexpectedly and hurriedly relocate once again, this time to central Florida, where it fell to me to settle her affairs and sell the house where I'd grown up. That became my job for the next ten months, and my work on the novel gradually trickled to a stop as I processed my grief and sorted through my mother's belongings. She and I had been estranged for most of my adult life, and despite being her only child, I had not counted on inheriting anything from her. But as it turned out, I had. For the first time in our life together, my husband and I didn't need to worry about money quite so much, and we had the luxury of taking some time off to decide what we wanted to do and where we wanted to go from here.

It didn't take us long to make up our minds; we knew now "what it means to miss New Orleans", and by this time (October 2008), things had been essentially back to normal in the city for quite some time. We'd kept in touch with Drs. C. and D. (well, Dr. D. in particular) and were still being told they wanted to work us back into the staff when openings became available (I noticed that the word used was *when,* not *if*). Dr. D. told me too that they "hardly ever" did declaw surgeries anymore; it wasn't like it *used* to be, and she hoped I was still considering coming back.

"Dr. C.'s really *mellowed* over the past few years, too!" she added, as if the claim about "hardly ever" declawing wouldn't be enough to lure me back. She knew me well enough to know exactly what I needed to hear the most.

We were back in New Orleans by Halloween, but it was several more months before the hospital found openings for both my husband and me (like always, they needed to be reduced to a *true* skeleton crew before they were willing to hire anyone else, but this time we could at least afford to wait.) I ended up taking a receptionist position again instead of being a tech this time, which was fine with me. I knew by now that I belonged more at the front desk than I did in the surgery suite; my mental health tended to be much better there.

Unfortunately, I would learn over the next year or so that none of Dr. D.'s claims were really true; Dr. C. was the same impatient, all-business, Very Important Doctor he'd always been, often brusque with cats and support staff, but always flashing warm and cheesy smiles at clients, colleagues, and business contacts. What bothered me more, though, was the fact that cats were still being declawed there fairly regularly- perhaps not quite as often as before, but certainly more than Dr. D. had led me to believe by saying "hardly ever".

The reduction- if any- in the number of declaw surgeries didn't seem to have anything to do with the hospital's practice philosophy or policies, which hadn't changed in the least. We still weren't teaching clients about the numerous humane alternatives to declawing, or even much about normal feline behavior and why they *need* to be able to scratch on approved items. We weren't recommending that they try vinyl nail caps or a few different kinds of scratching posts. Declawing simply wasn't being requested *quite* as often now, and I hoped that this was due to awareness beginning to spread about how harmful it is to cats.

I came to believe over that year that Dr. D's characteristically sunny and upbeat nature might be masking a coping technique known as "Pollyanna syndrome", which is form of denial in which people cling to an unflagging optimism rather than face hard truths36. I came to believe further that she was far from the only veterinary professional using such a coping mechanism. I still believe this.

On a number of occasions, the two of us got together after work to have a few glasses of wine, sometimes with a mutual friend along as well. She was still always making excuses for Dr. C's attitudes about declawing, his insensitive treatment of the staff, even his treatment of *her* (with his history of expecting her to give up her days off anytime they conflicted with *his* personal plans). She made excuses for him and the business manager (who'd replaced Tanya post-Katrina) continuing to lazily and cheaply hire techs who weren't working out well. And she still made excuses for herself, for going along with Dr. C's policy of offering declawing as an elective surgery. She could have told him that *he* would have to perform any declaw surgeries scheduled at his practice since *he* was the one who wanted to offer it, but instead she cheerfully did many of them herself, continuing with her old rationalization that "it means they'll get to stay in a good home". (In reality, it means nothing of the sort- ask virtually any shelter volunteer or rescue group how often they see declawed cats abandoned and in need of homes.)

One rationalization I could agree with Dr. D. about, though, was that our declaw surgery patients were better off with *her* doing it with a scalpel than they were with Dr. C. doing it Resco guillotine-style, particularly since with their painted metal parts and rubber grips, the nail trimmers were never autoclaved, the way real surgical instruments were. While the cats could do well or poorly after the surgery regardless of which doctor had done it or how, there was no denying that Dr. C's patients limped, seemed painful, and got infections more often than hers did. I couldn't understand why Dr. C. would want (or be allowed!) to cling to such an obviously outdated and inferior method of doing a surgery when he was supposed to be such a brilliant doctor, or why Dr. D. would think it was acceptable for him to do so when he placed such emphasis on his hospital being so advanced in every other way, but this was another thing she was able to excuse.

Older vets didn't have the time to learn every new technique that came along for doing everything, she said. Besides, there was no governing body in veterinary medicine that could force or compel vets to practice medicine in any particular way (and as far as I am aware, there still isn't today- not unless the corporate head office has *become* that governing body). Medicine was an *art* as well as a science, Dr. D. told me, and no doctor liked to step on a colleague's toes and dictate to them how to practice.

During one of those hangout sessions with Dr. D., drinking wine together, I actually ventured to suggest to her that if she wasn't really happy working for Dr. C., she didn't have to stay; I'd had dreams of investing my modest inheritance in opening a veterinary hospital of my own, but to do so legally, I would need a partner with a veterinary medical degree, and I'd love for her to be that partner.

She demurred, and I quickly pushed on: "I mean, whenever your contract is up again, or whatever would need to happen first, of course! And then we could run it the way *we* want to!"

She politely declined, saying she didn't really want the headaches of owning and running a business on top of practicing medicine. (This is a common sentiment in the veterinary world, and a major reason why it's become so easy in the past few years for corporations to take over so many independent veterinary hospitals as their owners sell out in greater and greater numbers. The CEOs' dazzling claim is that "we let vets focus on veterinary medicine, not management", but the danger in taking management decisions out of the hands of DVMs is that corporate "number crunchers" will always be more concerned about the financial bottom line than anything else- including patient care- no matter what they say.)

"Business is what Dr. C.'s good at," she went on. "He's a businessman." She finished off her glass of wine and poured another. "And an academic, but that's why he needs me to do the touchy-feely-caring stuff. We make a good team that way."

I realized in that moment that- just like that- she had summed up everything about Dr. C. that had always bothered me. He was a businessman *first* and a feline medical specialist almost as an afterthought; feline medicine was just the means to his desired ends (and almost as if to demonstrate this, he'd even pursued specialized training in veterinary management from a business school *before* he pursued the feline medical specialty certification). Maybe he *was* a brilliant academician, but as Aristotle is believed to have said, educating the mind without educating the heart is no education at all- particularly in a profession that's supposed to be built on caring. Dr. C.'s actions and attitudes constantly indicated to me that he cared more about growing his business than he did about his patients, his staff, or his clients as human beings. He'd *never* struck me on an intuitive level as a sincerely caring veterinarian. He'd practiced with a corporate mindset from the very beginning (just like Dr. G. and countless others did and do). I realize now that pet parents must be doubly wary when choosing their animals' healthcare, because *some* corporate number crunchers can *also* have impressive veterinary medical degrees.

"Well... let me know if you ever change your mind," I said, feeling foolish and sad. It was awkward for a few minutes, but then the wine came to our rescue, and we never spoke about it again.

I don't remember exactly when or how I first heard about the Paw Project. I didn't spend much time online prior to the late 2000's, but at some point, I came across news of a ban on declawing cats in the city of West Hollywood, California, which had been passed in 2003. The Paw Project, a veterinarian-led educational nonprofit organization, had been behind the success of the ban, which was the first of its kind in the United States.

Hearing about this gave me renewed hope that the tide was beginning to turn, that public opinion was beginning to change, though there was still a very long way to go. I believed then and still believe today that banning declawing in the United States is necessary, and a desirable goal. There are still too many DVMs in the U.S. who go about it the way that Dr. C. and Dr. G. did, blithely ruining cats' lives for quick and easy revenue, and vets who view this mutilating procedure as "no big deal" will not stop *using* it as a source of revenue until and unless they are legally *compelled* to stop- or they retire.

I believed Dr. D. when she said things like "Declawing is going to go away eventually", or "it's going to fall by the wayside". But I didn't want to just sit around waiting for that to happen anymore. I couldn't keep trying to be like Temple Grandin, forever trying to make trauma less traumatic for animals when I believed it *was* possible to eliminate the source of that trauma altogether. I thought it was part of our job (or at least, it *should* be part of our job- *to prevent and relieve animal suffering*, remember?) to help bring the change about ourselves- like Dr. Jennifer Conrad, the DVM who'd founded the Paw Project. It was heartening to know that "my tribe" of veterinary professionals actually *might* be out there somewhere willing to fight the good fight, even if they were in far-away places like California.

Through following the Paw Project, I learned about other things I could do to help end declawing *outside* of the hospital. If I was prohibited from talking to clients about more humane alternatives when they called to schedule their cats for declaw surgery... well, nobody could stop me (on my own time) from writing or phoning lawmakers in California, where efforts were underway by the Paw Project and their supporters to duplicate the West Hollywood ban on declawing in seven other cities, including some of the largest like Los Angeles and San Francisco. I remember once even writing to Arnold Schwarzenegger- who was serving as the governor of California at the time- about supporting the bans. *That* was a letter I could never have anticipated in a million years that I would write- asking "The Terminator" to help terminate declawing!

Nor could anyone stop me from signing and circulating petitions on social media or posting educational articles. Nobody could stop me from wearing a T shirt around town with the Paw Project's logo, which at the time depicted a human hand with the fingertips severed, and the slogan "If you're for declawing cats, raise *your* hand."

For the full story of the Paw Project's early efforts beginning in California and their subsequent battle with the California Veterinary Medical Association which did *not* appreciate those efforts, see their self-produced and self-titled 2013 documentary. As a result of the CVMA's lobbying for "a ban on bans", California did not become the first state to outlaw declawing completely; that honor went to New York in 2019, with Maryland becoming the second state to prohibit it in 2022. Virginia came next in July of 2024 (although the Virginia law unfortunately passed with an exploitable loophole, fought for and won by the Virginia Veterinary Medical Association). Cities with jurisdictional bans now include Washington, D.C.; Austin, TX; Madison, WI; Denver, CO; St. Louis, MO; Pittsburgh and Allentown, PA; and the original eight California cities. Bills in several other states have been introduced and reintroduced. But the movement to educate the public and protect cats *still* has a long way to go, twenty-one years after its initial success- and staunch opposition from the veterinary establishment is still the chief reason for this. Organizations like the AVMA- which exist to further the business interests of veterinarians, *not* animal welfare- seem determined to cling to declaw surgeries for as long as they possibly can. Not even the so-called "Cat Friendly Practices" established by the American Animal Hospital Association have necessarily eschewed declawing cats in 2024, since this is not a requirement for certification, although a similar initiative known as "Fear Free" *does* prohibit declawing in its certified practices. The Paw Project's work is ongoing, and includes a second documentary about declawing, planned for release in 2024 and entitled "American Cats: The Good, The Bad, and The Cuddly".

Dr. C. must have gotten wind of some of what I was doing; I didn't exactly make any of it a secret. If the tension between the two of us when we were forced to interact at work felt thicker, I neither cared nor acted as if I noticed. The more subtle warnings (as well as *not* so subtle!) that I received from the business manager about "misrepresenting" the hospital or its services, the more determined I was to keep speaking up (to anyone who would listen) about why declawing is wrong.

My days there were numbered again, and I knew it again. But this time I didn't have to be so terrified of losing my job, thanks to my mother. Ironically, though, one of the things she and I had always argued about was just how much I should be willing to put up with at a job that supplied a steady paycheck. "Principles are expensive," she'd always say. But I still thought they were worth having.

And here's the thing: I *did* put up with a lot; all of us did. When I finally gave up and left veterinary jobs, it wasn't because of the long hours that could be both emotionally and physically grueling- if not downright *hazardous* at times. It wasn't because of how often I would get called in on my days off or kept at work longer in the evening than I'd said I could stay. It wasn't because of the "demanding" clients or the relatively low pay, both of which always came with the territory. It was because I could no longer stand by and watch patients suffering needlessly (in *any* way, even if the doctors thought it was minor) while my hands were tied. Or it was because I made too much of a nuisance of myself by having the audacity to expect things to be done the *right* way- that is, the way I would want them done if I was the client, or if I was the *patient*. (And of course, in the case of Dr. Z.'s hospital, I technically hadn't left at all; it had simply been whisked out from under me!)

So I could see the writing on the wall again now, but before I left this time, I wanted to get some documentation of the kind of trauma we would so often see with cats recovering from declaw surgeries- the blood-spattered cages, the agonized faces, the poor chewed toe stumps. I thought that there were *very* few clients who would still want their cats declawed if they could see that such things happened to others, instead of being told that "most do just fine".

My husband and I each started bringing a small digital camera with us to work, hidden in a deep trouser pocket or in my purse. Since I worked at the front desk and he worked in the kennel, we were often the first staff members to arrive on the premises and open the hospital. Yes, you read that right: it was routine policy at that time for the first staff on the premises to be the receptionists (to wait on the clients and answer the phones) and the kennel staff (to start eliminating anything unsightly or any unpleasant odors before the clients started arriving). The *last* people usually scheduled to arrive were the techs and doctors- the very staff who would be the most immediately needed by any patient having an emergency first thing in the morning. It was another example of appearances being prioritized over actual patient care in a million little ways our clients had no way of knowing about. The reception area was always immaculate; clients could never tell when there was a cat languishing upstairs in what looked like a miniature abattoir the morning after a declaw procedure.

My husband had by this time been pressed into service as an extra pair of hands in the treatment area or exam room so many times that all our co-workers thought of him essentially as another tech, though that wasn't the job he'd signed on to do. So he had seen and cleaned up his share of blood-coated declaw recovery cages by now, too, and found it as stomach-turning as I did. He wanted to help. We knew that between the two of us, it wouldn't be that long before we could get some pictures that might be worth thousands of words. We got them in the summer of 2010.

CHAPTER ELEVEN

It was my day off and I was trying to sleep in when Dr. C. phoned me at home in an absolute rage. I knew immediately that he must have seen the photos I'd posted on my personal Facebook page the evening before: two declaw patients recovering in the hospital, their bedding and bowls covered with a fine blood spray. The scenes weren't as gory looking as many worse ones I'd witnessed, but both cats had been stable enough that I hadn't needed to intervene myself, so I'd been glad about that. I wasn't keen to see more suffering just so that I could document it. What I didn't understand right away was *how* Dr. C. had seen the photos; while I had a few co-workers as Facebook "friends", Dr. C. was definitely not one of them. (OK, yes, I was still relatively new to social media at the time, and I was naive.)

Dr. C. was hurling accusations at me; the one I mainly remember is that I was attempting "a malicious attack on his business". He hurled threats too, to the effect that if I didn't delete the photos from Facebook within 24 hours, I would be sorry because this was "actionable".

"I'm not attacking your business," I told him. "I'm just trying to show people how this hurts cats." (And truly: if I had *meant* my actions as an attack on his business, I wouldn't have made sure that there was *nothing* anywhere in my Facebook profile or in the photos themselves which plainly *identified* him or his business. If he took me to court, he would effectively "out" himself. I wasn't trying to harm him or gain anything. I was simply trying to get salient information to the public about a controversial veterinary procedure, in the only way I knew how. I didn't even have that many Facebook friends; this was long before being an "influencer" was something a person could viably do as a career. *These* days he's retired, but even if that were not the case, my motivation would remain the same in writing this book; my goal here is to help cats and their caregivers avoid common pitfalls in the veterinary world... *not* to attack any DVM in my story. It just so happens that one of those pitfalls- in my experience- is the existence of DVMs who may not be all that they seem.)

"I don't hurt cats! I only declaw them to keep them in their homes!" he spat through the phone, prompting me to remind him that all of his own cats were also declawed. As I said it, I realized that he probably viewed his own cats as little more than props to bolster his image- because after all, how many veterinarians have no pets of their own?

He didn't miss a beat. "*Yes,* my cats are declawed, because I have a *lot* of expensive stuff in my house that I don't want them *tearing up,* which is why nine out of ten people want their cats declawed!"

"Nice attitude for their *doctor* to have," I shot back.

"These cats are fine! *You* are *NOT* a doctor, and *you don't know what you're talking about*!" He was almost screaming. "You were hired to do a job, and if you don't believe in declawing cats, you should be bagging groceries, not working in a veterinary hospital! Not *MY* veterinary hospital!"

"That's *one* thing we can agree on," I said with a bitter laugh.

In the end, I capitulated and took the photos down, but a few of the right people had seen them in the short time they'd been on my profile, and this led to me being put in touch with the Paw Project. They wanted to use the photos in their previously mentioned documentary, which had already been in production for some time by then. Of course, I was thrilled to be able to help, and thrilled to know that now those pictures would have a better chance of being seen by the world than I would ever have been able to give them on my own.

To date, it remains the thing I am proudest of having done in my life, and I would absolutely do it again. My only regret is that I didn't do it sooner- as soon as I realized how wrong declawing was, in fact- and that I didn't do it *better:* smarter, more carefully, and with a lot more documentation compiled when I was done. I could have gotten so much more.

I could have gotten so much more.

And so, the summer of 2010 was the last time that either my husband or I worked in a veterinary medical setting. After we were both summarily dismissed, we assumed our names would be mud in the local veterinary community, and we felt like simply focusing on our *own* cats- both of whom really *were* entering their senior years by then- and *getting to be the clients* for a change.

I was really looking forward to this. The reader might think that the pets of veterinary professionals get *the best* healthcare, and I'm sure this is probably true in many cases. And I always believed that my favorite DVMs to work with were also the best ones available to me in my area. But everywhere I worked, staff pets were generally tended to as the *last* priority of the day, after all client pets and all appointments were seen, unless it was an emergency. (I'm sure this is also the policy in many other hospitals.)

Furthermore, we weren't permitted to schedule actual appointments for our own pets on our days off; those precious appointment slots were strictly reserved for clients, and to get our own kids seen, we'd have to bring them to work with us in the morning and keep them caged in the hospital all day, typically until we went home in the evening. Sometimes, if the day had gone *particularly* off the rails, our kids might end up sitting in cages all day without being seen by the doctor at all, and we'd have to try again another day. This always added an extra layer of stress to our workdays as we sympathized with our own babies, who always found the situation extremely confusing. And as for getting to have an uninterrupted conversation with the doctor about whatever might be going on with our own pets? I almost *never* had that luxury- not that I thought it should have been considered one. Does a mother with a human child consider *her* child's healthcare a luxury? Does she consider having the opportunity to discuss her child's condition with her child's doctor to be a luxury or a need?

I'd long wondered if the support staff members of pediatricians had to go through similar travails trying to get their own children seen; I still have no real idea, but I'd hazard a guess that this is highly dependent on individual cases, whereas in veterinary medicine my impression is that it tends to be more of a norm. Of course, simply *having* pets is still considered a luxury in our society, unlike having human children, despite the fact that younger generations- notably, millennials and Gen Z- are increasingly thinking of their pets more genuinely like "children" and themselves more like true "parents" to them, the way I've always done (and the way many of us in vet med have always done).

"The shoemaker's children always go barefoot," I remember one of the doctors telling me once, when I'd been wringing my hands over the way Merlin or Malachai had been crying in their cage. I don't recall which doctor that was, but it certainly hadn't made me feel any better, especially when my cats were there because they seemed under the weather.

So, yes- I was looking forward to being the client now. To be more accurate, I was looking forward to *my cats* finally getting to be *the patients* for a change- the precious *revenue bringing* patients, that is; the ones with humans who paid the full price for *all* services and recommended products. The *real* patients, not just two charity cases the doctor was obligated to see at a discount. (If I sound bitter here, perhaps I am somewhat. The companion animals of veterinary support staff members feel the same pain when unwell, the same fear and stress in the hospital as any other patient does, and they do not deserve lesser consideration or empathy because of who their humans are or how much the bill will be. For that matter, nor do the staff members on whose labor the entire practice survives deserve less consideration than a paying client does when their own pet is ill. But that was my consistent experience, and my understanding is that it's not uncommon.)

I'd hoped that Dr. D. and I would remain friends after "the incident" and she could still be my cats' doctor (on a house call basis! And we could hang out and drink wine together afterward!), but in that I suppose I was being naive again. Besides her loyalty to Dr. C., the two cats in the photos I'd taken had both been *her* surgical patients, so I imagine she may have viewed my actions as a personal attack on her, as well. She never responded to the text messages I sent her trying to explain myself; we never saw or spoke to each other again. But it was never about her, and it was never about my personal dislike of Dr. C. It was always and only about showing people how declawing harms cats... which was something *their doctors* were unwilling to do.

So, if my kids couldn't see Dr. D. anymore, the next logical choice for me seemed to be our hospital's other main competitor in the metro area- the one other feline-exclusive hospital; the one from which we'd inherited a couple of techs in the past. While they'd described this clinic as having many of the same staffing and efficiency problems as I'd always experienced in my own jobs, I figured I could only give it a try from the client's side of the desk and see what kind of impression I got for myself. I couldn't let my (now undeniably aging) boys go without healthcare, and since their needs were becoming more complex, I really wanted them to benefit from the specialized knowledge that *cat* vets have. So that's how we met "Dr. P".

She wasn't the first doctor we saw at the new hospital; that was her employer, the owner and founder of the clinic, "Dr. M". I'd been disappointed when I didn't feel that "click" with Dr. M. which had always helped me zero in on the doctor that I wanted for my cats. There had always been at least one, wherever I was working, who'd always had just a little more patience with my boys (and with my many questions). Dr. M. was gentle and respectful with my hissing little Merlin, but I hadn't found her to be a good listener during our first appointment. She seemed to enter the exam room with an idea already formed (based on the tech's intake notes) about what she was going to recommend, and it was difficult to get a word in edgewise, either to ask a question or to supply her with more pertinent information. She exuded an air of quiet but firm authority, and I could easily imagine her running this hospital in rigid ways that made little sense to anyone besides herself, like Dr. F. used to do. I thought I could see why the techs who'd "defected" from her clinic to ours may not have liked her much. But I wasn't dissuaded yet. I decided to ask for the other doctor at our next appointment and try again.

In contrast, Dr. P. was quick to cede the floor to her client when she could see I had something to say, and she seemed *eager* to listen. The more I could tell her about what was going on with my cats, the better she could feel about her potential diagnosis. I felt like an active partner in my children's healthcare, the way I wanted to feel, the way clients always *should* feel at their vet clinic; I didn't feel talked down to, the way I had with Dr. M. I could appreciate that the differences between them were probably mainly generational; Dr. M. had graduated and received her license before I'd been born, while Dr. P. was- like Dr. D.- much closer to my own age (in fact, for the first time in my life, I suspected I'd met a DVM who might even be slightly *younger* than me). She didn't strike me as inexperienced, however. I felt the "click" with her. And Merlin- my fractious little "problem child" with almost every other vet- actually seemed *relaxed* in her presence!

Dr. P. became my cats' doctor for the next five years- the final third of my boys' lives. It was she who helped me begin to overcome my terror of anesthetic procedures for them (which I'd never quite recovered from after the incident with Dr. G. and Malachai) and somewhat belatedly address their dental issues. It was Dr. P. who wrote letters for me recommending medical exemptions for my boys from their legally required rabies vaccines due to their advancing age, exclusively indoor lifestyle, and medical conditions. And it was Dr. P.

who, with great compassion and sensitivity, guided me twice through the most difficult part of being a companion animal caregiver: the goodbyes.

By that time, Dr. P. had become the owner of the hospital when Dr. M. retired, and she'd instituted some wonderful new policies. Under her leadership, the hospital had stopped declawing patients (!!!), and now offered clients the option of at-home euthanasia services when that painful time arrived. While every person and every pet are different, I believe that having the *option* to say goodbye in the comfort and privacy of one's own home is extremely valuable, particularly with cats. (In my experience, most cats do better in house call appointments in general for most of their healthcare needs, but few brick-and-mortar clinics today offer this service.)

There were several times over those five years when I considered applying for a job at Dr. P.'s hospital. I could see, even as a client, that the staff there seemed to consist of a loyal and stable few who remained there the whole time while many others passed in and out of the Great Revolving Door, just like at every clinic where I'd worked. So, this hospital was not immune to it either (I'd never really believed that Dr. M.'s personality could have been *entirely* to blame), and I imagined that working there would most likely be very much like what I was used to. And I just didn't want to do it. I didn't *need* to work at my vet's office anymore; I could afford my cats' treatment on my own. And as my cats lived out their twilight years, I thought they deserved finally to no longer have to smell the scent of *other* cats all over me when I came home every day. *This* shoemaker's children were not going to go barefoot any longer.

I often wondered if one reason I was able to let go and trust Dr. P. and her staff was because I *wasn't* working there and never really got to see what things were like "in the back". As the saying goes, you don't know what you don't know, and I was sure that if I *did* know, I'd probably have more reservations. The staff turnover that I could observe without even trying told me more than I wanted to know already, but I let Merlin and Malachai be my guides. I observed them very carefully whenever they were returned to me from "the back"; Merlin in particular- with his high-strung nature- would let me know if something especially scary had happened to him or near him. He would never be *happy* in a vet clinic, but based on his behavior there, I felt I could trust the place. I really liked the tech who usually worked with Dr. P., as well (she was going to be *licensed!*), and I felt good about her looking out for the patients there.

Both before the Covid-19 pandemic and again after social distancing policies were relaxed, I've seen some people on social media advising pet parents *never* to allow their animal to be taken out of their sight at the vet clinic, and I think this advice is somewhat problematic, even despite all the reasons the reader may feel I've been listing for clients to be wary.

As a former veterinary professional, I agree with the clinics when they say that sometimes, it truly is necessary, and likewise, there are times when it would simply not be in the best interests of patients to allow clients "in the back" where treatments or surgeries are underway. Nowadays, I also can't fault *any* business or workplace for trying to maintain a diligent Covid mitigation policy- although I believe that by now, there are probably ways to do this while still allowing transparency about the hospital's daily operations, and transparency is needed.

I agree with the clients when they want to be heard regarding whether or not their pet will do better with them in the room, and when they want the opportunity to see the area where their animal will be kept while they're in the hospital- with circumstances permitting, of course. I agree with them when they worry that if "the pandemic is over", then veterinary clinics still clinging inflexibly to a lockdown-era level of keeping clients at a distance could be hiding something questionable[37].

Prior to Covid, the policy at my old workplaces was to schedule a clinic tour as an appointment for any client who was interested, and that way we could schedule routine surgeries around it, or move it to another time if need be due to an emergency coming in. Some clients weren't satisfied with this and expected us to grant them an all-access pass at any moment they chose, but this isn't permitted in human medicine either, and for good reasons. I felt then and still feel that a policy like those we had makes a good compromise.

After our boys had both crossed the Rainbow Bridge- just ten months apart- my husband and I felt unmoored, at a crossroads. Our kids had been the center of our world, just like any couple's children are the center of theirs. We decided we wanted a major change of scenery; it was too painful to stay in the last home we'd shared with our boys, and when our lease ended, we decided to take some time to do some extended traveling.

For years we'd dreamed of visiting Colorado, and we decided now was the time. We packed our furniture and most of our belongings into a storage unit, except for our clothes and a few other items we could use in hotel rooms, and for a few months we lived on the road, traveling mostly around Colorado, but taking a few excursions to other states as well. It was very therapeutic, but *very* expensive to be living what's called "van life" today, but *without* the van to live in! Clearly, we couldn't keep doing it forever, and we needed to decide where to settle down again. We didn't feel ready to leave Colorado, so we decided to look at the town of Pueblo, which we knew almost nothing about other than its affordability when compared to most other towns and cities along Colorado's Front Range.

In December of 2016 we moved into a newly renovated apartment in Pueblo, and I decided I wanted to adopt another cat. That's how we ended up finding our little girl a few months later.

CHAPTER TWELVE

My husband and I quickly learned that Pueblo did not suit us as well as we'd hoped- it didn't suit us well at all, in fact. But the town did have a no-kill animal shelter that impressed me with its cleanliness, its progressive design (adoptable cats lived in suites of miniature rooms in small groups, not locked in cages), and its alignment with many of my own opinions about companion animal care.

It was there that we met Spooky- one of the quietest, shyest, and sweetest cats I've ever known. "Spooky" was what they were calling her at the shelter, but I can't recall if they said whether she'd come in with that name or they'd given it to her. No matter; we would be keeping it, both because it suited her so well (she was easily spooked) and because I believe adopted animals deserve to keep a name they've grown accustomed to or to which they respond.

The shelter told us that Spooky was about three years old, since their vet had placed her at about one year of age upon intake; she'd already spent almost two whole years at the shelter waiting to be adopted. As an adult-sized cat who was timid and withdrawn as well as having a black coat, the odds would never be in her favor when it came to finding a home that was a good fit for her, especially in a town like Pueblo, where everyone seemed to have dogs or horses, but nobody seemed to understand cats- or to *want* to understand them. Our original plan had been to adopt a much older cat if one was available, but after hearing Spooky's story and how long she'd been there, we couldn't say no to her.

According to the shelter, she had been living in what sounded very much like a meth lab, which had been raided by law enforcement officers who found that their suspect had eluded them and left Spooky abandoned in the house. We were told that "we had tests done to be sure none of the fumes from that place affected her", but the scanty medical records the shelter could provide mentioned absolutely nothing about this. (I always made sure to mention this history to every new vet who saw Spooky, and although no diagnostic test ever did turn up anything that was obviously related to it, I will always wonder how much "that place" did affect her.) I had a difficult time even confirming her vaccine status, since there were several spots in the paperwork where the dates seemed to be conflicting. We knew that she hadn't been spayed yet when she arrived at the shelter and it had been done there (her adoption fee was $20 more than other cats as a result, giving her an even *worse* chance at being adopted), but that was virtually all the medical history we had. In all likelihood, her medical history was probably essentially just beginning when we adopted her.

I became concerned immediately when I noticed streaks of blood in her stools, although I remembered what Dr. F. had been fond of saying about blood in the stool not being an emergency, and colitis can be relatively common in animals who come from a stressful shelter environment. Spooky's shelter also allowed groups of cats to share litterboxes, so it was fairly likely she could have picked up an intestinal parasite, which would be easily treatable. She was eating well and seemed to feel fine, so I knew we didn't have an emergency, but it wasn't something to ignore, either. I started looking for a new vet in earnest.

The first one I tried was a mixed practice in Pueblo, and the option that had sounded the best to me without having to drive more than an hour away. I didn't "click" with them at all; they were the epitome of my experiences at mixed cat-and-dog practices, where cats were distinctly thought of and treated as "second class citizens". As soon as the doctor heard that I'd been a vet tech, she seemed to expect me to then become *her* tech when she was working with Spooky- an extra, experienced pair of hands for free, just like vets always seemed to want. I tried to explain that I'd just adopted this cat, I was still trying to establish a bond with her, and I didn't want her to associate me with too many unpleasant experiences right away. The doctor was visibly irritated at this. We didn't go back.

The closest feline specialty hospital was north of Pueblo in Colorado Springs. Going there would mean traveling over an hour each way, but I hoped it would be worth it; the place sounded amazing to me- like the kind of cat hospital I would have tried to open myself, if Dr. D. had taken me up on my offer. They actually referred to themselves as a "feline healthcare center". They didn't declaw; instead, they sold quality scratching posts in the lobby and taught clients how to use them correctly for the best results. In many ways, they were like a dream come true for me.

Unfortunately, *all* their clients seemed to feel the same way, and due to their status as the one and only feline specialty veterinary hospital serving clients like me who came to them from all over a huge area, it was always near impossible to get an appointment right away, or a phone call back from the doctors when I had concerns or questions. I was experiencing a pandemic-level degree of difficulty accessing quality care for my cat- years before the pandemic. Spooky's doctor and I kept in touch mainly through e-mail. I liked her, but thought the clinic was stretching itself far too thin to serve all their patients adequately. It was yet another version of the same old problem.

Meanwhile, my husband and I were realizing that we really did not want to stay in Pueblo any longer, particularly after learning that a substantial portion of the town had been designated as an EPA "Superfund site" where the ground was contaminated with toxic waste. Rent in Colorado Springs- closer to Spooky's vet- seemed a little too rich for our blood after our expensive "van life" adventure, and several attempts I'd made to get a job at vet hospitals in both towns had for the first time yielded nothing (forcing me to wonder if I would ever be able to work in the field again after "the incident"- had I been blacklisted?).

We'd begun to miss New Orleans again, and I certainly missed Dr. P. and the great rapport I felt I'd had with her. So in the spring of 2018, we returned to the Crescent City and to Dr. P.'s hospital with Spooky.

Dr. P. seemed busier than I'd remembered, perhaps in part because in the couple of years we'd been away, she had become the president of the Louisiana Veterinary Medical Association. I was excited by this because I hoped it meant she could be a valuable ally in any effort to ban declawing or change the culture of the veterinary establishment in the state of Louisiana- though I never had an opportunity to broach this subject with her. I was nevertheless delighted to see her clinic's front door displaying a Paw Project decal (with its new, cuter logo featuring a bright-eyed cartoon kitty) indicating they were a "claw friendly" practice, and I didn't mind too much that Dr. P. didn't seem to be quite as available as she'd been in the past. It was still an improvement over the Colorado Springs hospital in that regard. My favorite tech was still there, and had followed through on her plan to become formally licensed. So I felt pretty good about coming back, overall.

I felt good about it until June of 2020, when Dr. P. announced that she had decided to relocate to the Pacific Northwest to be near family members there, and that Dr. M. would be returning from retirement and taking charge of the hospital again.

Dr. P. wasn't one of the veterinary professionals joining the "mass exodus" from the field that was beginning to be apparent in 2020; in fact, her announcement went on to say that once settled, she planned to pursue the same rigorous board certification in feline specialty medicine that Dr. C. had attained. I was happy about that, but very sad that New Orleans- and Spooky- would be losing her. We said goodbye to her the following month.

When Dr. M. resumed running the hospital, I almost immediately noticed fees beginning to increase for many products and services- sometimes rather sharply from what they had cost when Dr. P. was still there. It had been a long time since I'd been a regular reader of the veterinary industry magazines, and I couldn't even begin to imagine how the chaotic news of 2020 (and now 2021) was affecting businesses of *all* kinds, but I had the clear impression that Dr. M. was purposely trying to increase revenue at her hospital now.

I thought it was perhaps understandable for her to want to recoup some pandemic-related losses, but it was also now feeling just as difficult to access care for Spooky as it had felt in Colorado Springs-*worse* even, because whereas the Colorado Springs doctor had been good at communicating with me by e-mail (and occasionally with a precious phone call), Dr. M. routinely delegated this to her receptionists (when I received a response at all!), reserving direct access to *her* for appointment times only. That would have been fine... had I been able to get quality answers to my questions from her receptionists. But as was typical for most DVMs to do in my experience, she *also* failed to sufficiently educate or empower her staff to be able to answer most questions from clients. Thus, whenever I had a concern- even a minor one- I was expected to schedule an appointment, pay an exam fee, and- the part that really bothered me- put undue stress on Spooky when she didn't really need to be examined, just so I could have a chance to discuss her progress and treatment directly with her doctor. It made it hard to *perceive the value* that should have justified the higher fees Dr. M was charging, and it was becoming more than frustrating.

In the interest of fairness, perhaps I was judging Dr. M. just a little harshly, based on the way I was used to the veterinary world operating prior to Covid. While it was true that Dr. P. had still been able to return e-mails and phone calls *herself* in a timely manner several months into the pandemic in 2020, I reasoned that Dr. M. had been forced out of retirement, after all. Maybe she was just having trouble keeping up with the faster-than-ever pace. I tried an appointment with her new associate, a "Dr. T." who was much younger, but I didn't "click" with her either, and communication was still a major problem. It seemed to simply be the new hospital policy to eliminate the kind of supportive partnership with clients that Dr. P. had always fostered to maximize her patients' chances for success, with follow-up conversations built into her case management style. In contrast, now I felt very much on my own. Still concerned? Make another appointment!

Maybe it was due to the stresses of the pandemic, but maybe this was also the way Dr. M. had always been; I'd never really dealt with her after that very first appointment with Merlin, so I didn't know. What I *did* know was that now, beyond lacking the "click" with Dr. M., I was beginning to think that she might be prioritizing the business side of the hospital over the caring side, like Dr. C. had always done. She *had* continued to declaw cats up until her retirement, as far as I knew; it had taken Dr. P.'s leadership to end that practice, and I would be lying if I said that this hadn't been a factor in my perception of Dr. M. right from the beginning.

When she recommended a surgical procedure for Spooky which carried some significant risks and was considered somewhat radical- for a condition which didn't seem to warrant such aggression- I balked. We'd recently had to adjust our estimation of Spooky's age, since in the four years she'd been with us, she'd seemed to be collecting more and more age-related issues. When a bloodwork panel and urinalysis revealed her to have developed chronic kidney disease, we knew she had to be older than we'd been told- and I knew that having compromised kidneys automatically made anesthesia more of a risk. I hesitated and vacillated about scheduling the surgery; Dr. M. responded by becoming more insistent, and I began to feel pressured.

One day I was venting to a friend who'd spent some time working as a receptionist at a Banfield hospital located not far from where I'd been taking Spooky to Dr. P. (and then Dr. M.). It was from my friend that I learned that Dr. K. had been the main DVM at that Banfield for some years now- kindly Dr. K., who I remembered fondly from working together years before. I jumped at the chance to get Spooky a second opinion from a DVM I knew personally and trusted, even if it had to be at *Banfield,* where I never would have imagined myself choosing to take any pet of my own for treatment. It would be great to see Dr. K. again, too, I thought. So I made Spooky an appointment.

It felt strange to be dropping her off at the back of a PetSmart store where- despite the Banfield reception desk- it didn't really look or feel like a veterinary hospital to me. I didn't see a single other cat being dropped off besides Spooky; just dog after dog after dog. Normally this wouldn't have boded well, but I knew Dr. K. was great with cats; gentle, patient, and sensitive to their body language. I'd watched her examine enough of them to know. I wished intensely that I'd been allowed to schedule an office visit rather than having to drop Spooky off, but I well understood the clinic's reasons for denying clients this due to Covid- even though many businesses had begun to relax their pandemic policies by this time (February 2022). In contrast, Dr. M. had *never* suspended office visits at her hospital, even during the most dangerous heights of the pandemic, and I'd had mixed feelings about that as well, since cats are also at risk of contracting Covid 19.

As I was checking Spooky in, I couldn't help noticing the whiteboard on the wall behind the reception desk, where the day's patients were listed- over 30 of them. And the day hadn't even really begun yet; when I was working in vet hospitals, we *always* knew that once the phones started ringing in the morning, we would get even busier than the schedule was showing. I nervously asked the receptionist how many doctors were working that day.

"Oh, we just have Dr. K. today," she said cheerfully, and my heart sank a little. I remembered what "Dr. K. days" had been like when we worked at the feline hospital together. The time and care she took with all her patients and clients was what I loved about her, but it did tend to make her undeniably *slow*. I couldn't believe Banfield was giving her that many patients to see all by herself in one day. I didn't see how it was all going to get done.

It didn't go badly that first time as I recall; Dr. K. had Spooky ready for me to pick up before the end of the business day, much earlier than

I'd expected, and she seemed no worse for wear (although it could be hard to tell sometimes how Spooky might be feeling; when frightened, she had a tendency to simply freeze in place).

Dr. K. agreed wholeheartedly with me that Spooky was not the greatest candidate for the surgery Dr. M. was recommending, and that it was reasonable and prudent of me to hold off and monitor her condition for the time being. The risk-to-potential-benefit ratio wasn't good enough in her opinion at this time, particularly since she'd also detected a heart murmur that Dr. M. had never mentioned to me, which made Spooky an even poorer surgical candidate than I'd thought. It was extremely validating to hear this, and at that point I saw no real reason to continue going back to Dr. M. anymore. I transferred Spooky's records over to Banfield.

This would have been the time for Dr. K. to tell me that it might have been in Spooky's best interests to maintain a relationship with Dr. M.'s hospital as well. She knew that her Banfield clinic was practicing in a very different way than we had at the feline specialty hospital; she knew they didn't have advanced capabilities such as ultrasound diagnostics, and they didn't do a lot of complicated, aggressive case management, as she and I had done for so many patients together in the past. They were much more of a *clinic* than a true *hospital,* and although these words are sometimes used interchangeably (and I've been guilty of that here as well), there is a difference.

Everything I'd seen and experienced in veterinary medicine had taught me that the quality and standard of care was dependent on the DVM doing the caring more so than the facility in which they did it, and I had no reason to think that Dr. K. had changed significantly from when I'd known her before, even though it had somehow been almost *twenty years* since we'd worked together. But Banfield was simply not the right healthcare facility for a cat who had unexpectedly turned out to have entered her senior years, who was already diagnosed with one progressive and life-limiting disease and who might have potentially been developing another one (since there were several areas of her anatomy that we were monitoring for warning signs of cancer). I believe now that Dr. K. should have realized from the start that Banfield wasn't up to Spooky's needs, and she should have been forthcoming with me about this. She knew all those things, but I did not.

Not until it was too late for me to make better decisions for my child.

Over the next fourteen months, our little girl seemed to be aging before our eyes, and we wondered whether the shelter had really miscalculated her age by that much, or if perhaps they'd deliberately misrepresented it, hoping to improve her chances for adoption. The irony in that was that it hadn't been necessary with us; adopting an older, "less adoptable" cat was what we'd set out to do. It was quite the emotional roller coaster to learn that our time with her would be much more limited than we'd believed. But I was determined to give her the best quality of life I possibly could, for as long as it was possible. We'd lost Merlin to chronic kidney disease (which affects 1 in 3 cats over the age of ten[38]), and I was trying to be very proactive about supporting Spooky's kidneys as much as possible, as early as possible. (Dr. M.'s constant brushing aside of these concerns in favor of discussing at length things which didn't worry me as much- or which I already understood- was typical of her inability to listen to her clients.) I took Spooky to see Dr. K. every two or three months to monitor her bloodwork, her urine specific gravity, and a problematic anal gland which had a history of abscesses (removing this gland was the delicate and somewhat risky surgery that Dr. M. had wanted to do, and discussing it was one of the things she prioritized over my concerns about Spooky's kidney health). Over time, Spooky began to display more and more anxiety around her vet visits- to the point that she became fearful whenever my husband would put on his shoes or pick up his car keys, because she automatically thought it meant we would be taking her to see the doctor. I increasingly began to doubt whether the frequent visits were truly worth it; they seemed to make no difference in her quality of life except to cause her stress.

Banfield never returned to offering real office appointments wherein the client could sit down and talk with the doctor in privacy; their version of a "sit-down appointment" only differed from a drop-off appointment in that the doctor agreed to see the pet within a given time frame. The pet still ended up "in the back" for at least a couple of hours, so particularly from Spooky's perspective, there was no real difference at all. And I still had to stand out in the open in the back of the PetSmart store, discussing my child's healthcare with her doctor in full view and earshot of the public, even when privacy was much desired.

The more visits we had, the more obvious it was to me that Dr. K. was having a lot of difficulty keeping up with her case load; the list of patients on the whiteboard for the day *always* stretched on for more than 30 names, and I realized that this was Banfield's business-as-usual; it hadn't just been a particularly crazy day the first time we'd come to see her. Communication from her became spottier and briefer, and I was increasingly forced to wonder whether Dr. K. had gotten my messages at all, or if she would manage to return my phone call or email before Banfield closed for the day and turned off their phones. It began to happen *so* consistently that I wondered if it was actually a Banfield *policy* that doctors were to wait until the end of the business day to return any messages from clients. That's fine in some cases, but with an aging, sick pet, a day's delay in being able to make an informed decision about their care can have serious consequences.

I wanted to be understanding. I *was* understanding. Nobody had to tell me how busy a veterinary hospital can get, and nobody had to tell me that Dr. K. was doing the best she could. I *knew* how it was;

how it had *always* been in veterinary medicine, *and* I knew about the effect of "a Dr. K. day"- so why didn't Banfield know it? Why didn't they make any effort to support a good doctor who was still trying to *be* a good doctor? Why were they piling so much on her plate? It began to go beyond frustrating me to making me angry. I couldn't believe that Dr. K. would have practiced in this way if given much choice about it.

At that time, I didn't realize the degree or scope of the pandemic's impact on the veterinary profession; my own coping mechanism during the height of Covid (and the surrounding political turmoil) was to avoid the news- any and *all* news- as much as possible, and so I didn't yet know about the surge in pet adoptions across the U.S. during lockdown or the "mass exodus" of DVMs and techs from the field in the previous couple of years. I blamed the typical veterinary medical mindset of trying to pack in too much business for your skeleton crew to be able to handle- the way almost every vet hospital I'd ever dealt with had *always* seemed to be doing, with one excuse or another. I surmised the problem was even worse at Banfield due to corporatization. And- as I stated at the beginning of this memoir- I still believe that I wasn't entirely wrong; the pandemic was *one* of the reasons veterinary medicine suddenly seemed to be struggling to keep up with demand everywhere, but I knew it was far from the *only* reason, the way it was seemingly being portrayed.

I knew as well that I was the kind of client that had always been considered "high maintenance" by veterinary staff. I was extremely engaged in my cats' lives and very invested in their care; I asked a *lot* of questions and came to every appointment armed with notebooks full of observations about their eating, sleeping, and elimination habits. (Being familiar with what's "normal" for your pet goes a long way towards early detection when something is *not* normal.) I always tried to be patient and respectful to the staff of any vet practice where I was a client, however, because I *did* understand all too well how difficult their jobs could be, and how much *more* difficult it could become when clients had unreasonable expectations. I didn't think I was being unreasonable when I wanted answers the same day regarding how to assess Spooky's end-stage quality of life, however.

Remember the pet caregiver from the beginning of my story- the one complaining on social media that her vet clinic was "broken" because she felt completely unsupported in navigating the complex and painful end-of-life issues unique to veterinary medicine? Yes... that was me.

The DVM who told me "Their practice is not broken if they're busy and making enough to live on" sounded just like Dr. C., who could have used a reminder that a veterinary hospital has a purpose *beyond* making a profit for its owner. When the DVM on social media accused me of being "just mad that they don't need to serve you to make a decent living", he didn't know how familiar I was with working in the veterinary industry, and thought he was talking to the average layperson client. He thought he was talking to a "Karen" as well- a spoiled consumer with a sense of entitlement; the kind we used to refer to as "a brown-dot client" all the way back at Dr. F.'s practice in Atlanta, where a color-coded system of tiny decals on the medical records would alert staff to clients who tended to be difficult, impatient, or unreasonable. (We had "red-dot patients" as well- those who might try to bite or scratch- and "green-dot clients", who were those with chronic financial constraints who would always need a detailed estimate for any recommended treatments.)

It astonished me that any DVM was willing to state things like that to a grieving client in a public forum- even Dr. C. had always known better than that. To be sure, I had certainly heard callous things come out of his mouth- as on one memorable occasion when he'd complained bitterly to Tanya that clients hadn't wanted to continue with his aggressive- and expensive- treatment plan for their elderly cat who was plainly dying. He'd learned they'd opted for private cremation after her passing and was quick to condemn their decisions: "They couldn't pay for her to stay alive, but they came up with the money for Heaven's Pets, now, *didn't they?*" But Dr. C. was always careful to never let his mask of congeniality slip when he was talking to a client's face. He was a businessman, after all, and that wouldn't be good for business. I suppose it might be different for a DVM these days when the client you offend isn't *your* client, but just *a* client- one of those "demanding, ungrateful" clients apparently driving veterinary professionals away in droves nowadays.

For me, the exchange with the DVM on social media just confirmed that what I'd been saying there was true- vet med *is* broken. The pandemic may have made the damage obvious, but if my story serves to accomplish nothing else, I hope it illustrates that the cracks have been there for a long, long time.

I even asked Dr. K. point blank if I was demanding too much of her time, and her careful response was that she did work for a high-volume clinic (as if I'd ever known there to be any *other* kind, at least since Dr. F. had retired!), and that there simply wasn't enough time in the day to give the time she wished to everyone. This made me recall the platitude about "the shoemaker's children" again; it occurred to me that she probably expected me to be more self-sufficient when it came to making decisions for Spooky, due to my years of working in hospitals. But ironically, all my experience had really taught me was just how many things can go wrong in medicine, without really educating or empowering me to feel that I could handle them if they *did* occur. I wasn't a doctor- not even close. I wasn't ever even a real nurse, although I was given the responsibilities of one, and was expected to step up and act like one. I still needed a doctor's advice for my child... but there was simply none to be had.

And I knew that- setting the pandemic aside- veterinary hospitals have never *had* to be run the way that Banfield was doing it. It's always been *possible* to allot adequate time for all patients to be seen and all clients' concerns to be addressed- but hospital management needs to make that their priority, and very few practice owners or managers are willing to do this anymore, in either human or veterinary medicine. It works against the *true* goal of for-profit healthcare, which *is* to be high-volume.

In the end, Dr. K. sent me back to Dr. M.'s hospital when Spooky and I had "reached the limit of what we can do for her here," and I realized that the doctor I'd worked side by side with for several years- and who I trusted more than any other DVM currently available to me- had no intention of seeing us through the end of Spooky's life. Instead, she was recommending that I take my child back to a doctor who hadn't seen Spooky or followed her case for over a year by this time, and whose opinion I hadn't fully trusted when she *had*.

I felt abandoned and betrayed. I felt *used* for as long as it was profitable, and then tossed out the door when my cat and I became too much work. But I was more upset about Spooky losing continuity of care than I was about any perceived slight to *me*. I tried a few more times to send questions to Dr. K. through e-mail, but she soon stopped responding to me entirely. I didn't want to think that she had done this deliberately; for all I knew, she might have expected me to return to Dr. M. promptly after getting the second opinion from her. But she never said a word to that effect, and I couldn't help wondering if the Dr. K. I thought I knew had changed- or if it was working at Banfield that had changed her.

Back at Dr. M.'s hospital, I got the distinct impression that she and Dr. T. actively resented my returning to them with Spooky a year after I'd declined to do the surgery Dr. M. had recommended. But the gland she'd wanted to remove still showed no signs of becoming cancerous, and I was glad now that I hadn't put Spooky through that surgery, since another one was potentially looming. One of the last things I'd been discussing with Dr. K. was an abdominal mass she'd thought she felt, and this had been what finally caused her to send us back to Dr. M.: Spooky officially had too many serious health problems for Banfield to manage any longer. I finally discovered the secret to getting a phone call back from Dr. M. when I volunteered to pay- at my own suggestion- a telehealth appointment fee for her to call me. (*"Please,"* I remember saying to the receptionist. *"Please, I'm begging here... can she PLEASE just call me back? I will HAPPILY PAY for her time!"* And suddenly, time was found in the schedule.)

An abdominal ultrasound (technology Banfield hadn't possessed) revealed the mass to be huge, and exploratory surgery to remove it was the recommendation, which Dr. M. and Dr. T. agreed upon. I think *exploratory surgery* is a term whose significance is underappreciated by the average person, who hasn't witnessed one. The incisions tend to be *massive,* sometimes essentially opening up the entire body cavity and spreading it wide to ensure that there are no other abnormalities to be found, and that the entire mass is removed. I'd been *horrified* the first time I watched one. They can be extremely hard on the patient and difficult to recover from, even for young and relatively healthy animals. I'd assisted with exploratory surgeries on geriatric cats with multiple system disorders like Spooky, and I'd assisted with euthanasia under the same circumstances, and I felt that euthanasia was the much kinder option. I knew that with Spooky's compromised kidneys, heart murmur, hypertension, and unknown actual age, there was a fair chance she might not even survive the surgery, and that was *not* the way I wanted her life to end.

The doctors didn't talk to me about any of these things, however. I doubt they were taking my veterinary experience into consideration when they failed to inform their client of all the risks to consider when deciding whether to go ahead with surgery. They really only presented me with one choice- THEIRS. In the end, the *only* reason I felt I was able to make the decision that I did- to allow Spooky to pass from this life in peace and comfort at home, rather than risking her dying on the surgery table (or soon afterward, in pain, as I'd seen with others) with her last conscious moments spent in abject fear- was because I had the same insider's knowledge of veterinary medicine that the doctors had... but which they *weren't sharing*.

Veterinarians reading this will probably say that doctors try to avoid overburdening their clients with too much information and making their decision more difficult, and while that is understandable, *they* need to understand that all clients are not the same, and for each one who wants the decision essentially taken out of their hands for them by the doctor, there is another like me, who wants to know *everything* they should consider. When in doubt, I think vets should simply *ask* their clients how much in-depth information they want to have.

Dr. M. had dropped at-home euthanasia service from her practice at some point after taking it back from Dr. P.; I had no idea if that was due to Covid or not. But at that point, I wouldn't have wanted either her or Dr. T. in my home with their thinly-disguised disapproval of my decision; I wouldn't have wanted them present in Spooky's final moments, and I wouldn't have wanted Dr. K. there, either. At least in the end, it didn't *matter* that I was forced to call a complete stranger to assist Spooky gently over the Rainbow Bridge instead of a trusted "other family doctor", because at that point, a stranger was the only DVM I felt I *could* trust.

I called Lap Of Love, the groundbreaking mobile veterinary hospice service founded in 2009, which now operates in well over half of the states in the country. They made scheduling the appointment as easy as it could be under the circumstances, and the doctor who saw Spooky for the last time was comforting and compassionate to our whole family. She told me that, all things considered, she would not have wanted to put Spooky through exploratory surgery either, had she been her caregiver, and that was important for me to hear, even if I couldn't hear it from our own veterinarian.

Just as every client is different, so is every patient, and I've seen pet parents debating whether it's better for our animals to have a stranger for their last vet appointment, or the person that they *recognize* as "the vet". Having done it both ways, with cats that had a similar level of anxiety surrounding having to see "the vet", I can honestly say that it didn't seem to make much difference, because they were ready to go, and they seemed to know in both cases that this person was there to help them.

CHAPTER THIRTEEN

Spooky left us at the end of May in 2023. Earlier in the month- on Mother's Day, in fact- I'd seen the news about the shooting at the Kentucky veterinary clinic that left one employee dead. Based on my own recent experiences with the veterinary world- no, scratch that; based on *all* my experiences with the veterinary world, I suddenly realized, but especially the recent ones- I thought I could understand the depth of the client's undoubted frustration (maybe even *desperation*), although it goes without saying that violence is not the answer.

And so, in between providing hospice care at home for Spooky- while she slept at my side- I started writing this memoir primarily *for her,* because my little girl who'd been let down by most of her doctors deserved to have her story told. For Spooky, for Malachai and Merlin; for Grendel, Missy, and Ralph; for every other patient I ever wished I could help more... and for all the ones currently needing vet care who I'll never know about... I felt I had to try to make some sense of all of this. I felt that I was mourning not only Spooky, but my ill-starred career in veterinary medicine... and maybe even veterinary medicine *itself* as I had always known it. During the writing process, I realized that my story/my children's stories/my patients' stories were also the stories of many other companion animals and veterinary professionals across the country, and I was writing this book for all of them as well.

So, what *is* the answer?

I am not the only one saying that #vetmedisbroken; I am not the only one who knows it. I *may* be the only one who believes that the very first crack was there from the profession's very beginning, when humans undertook medical care for their animals because it benefited *them*- the humans- and not the patients receiving the care.

I don't pretend to have all the answers to all the questions about how to reform or repair the profession in the 2020s so that it aligns more with what pet caregivers want from it today, but I think we need to start there, with its fundamental, first value. *Veterinary care should benefit the patient receiving it, first and foremost.* This leads directly into what I believe is the next most fundamental thing: "the prevention and relief of animal suffering" should be the very first priority- *not* expansion and profit. That's how I believed it was when I was a child who wanted to be a vet when she grew up. That's how pet parents believe it is, or how it should be. That's how we *want* it to be. That's the way for a veterinary hospital to truly be "your other family doctor". If the traditional idea of a "family doctor" for *anyone* still has a place in modern society, genuine *caring* needs to come first.

Perhaps I'm simply mourning a bygone era, however. For an impressively long time, veterinary medicine seemed- to me- the one field resistant to the insidious advancement of late-stage capitalism, holding out much longer than human medicine did in the United States. But increasingly now, the veterinary industry too is corporate rather than independent; a franchise rather than a family. (The independent hospital you've taken your pets to for years can even be taken over by a corporate entity without their clients ever being the wiser. In a particularly disingenuous trend, some hospitals will keep all signage and outward appearances exactly the same after transitioning to corporate control- to camouflage the fact that their services and hospital culture will inevitably be changing.) Increasingly, vet med is joining other industries in turning to technology rather than caring people to patch the longstanding holes in its healthcare teams, automating everything which can be automated and placing more and more hope in the promise of artificial intelligence to provide the perfect (and tireless) assistance to keep up with increased demand for services. To me, this doesn't feel like the right direction in which to go.

In early 2024 a survey was conducted by the veterinary practice management software company Digitail in partnership with the American Animal Hospital Association (AAHA). The survey asked

4000 respondents their opinions about AI in veterinary medicine and received answers from diverse voices across the industry. Approximately half the respondents were DVMs and technicians, but veterinary assistants, receptionists/CSRs, practice managers, business executives, students, and support staff in "other roles" were also included. Over 43% of them reported feeling either "somewhat optimistic" or "very optimistic" about AI in vet med, and almost 40% indicated an interest in incorporating AI tools into their practices in the near future.

Among the different categories of respondents, the DVMs and business executives were overall the most optimistic and enthusiastic about embracing AI, while veterinary technicians and respondents working in shelter medicine or for nonprofit organizations were the least optimistic and the most skeptical about AI in veterinary medicine39- and I personally find this rather telling. Perceived benefits to using AI tools include "more efficient resource allocation", "increased revenue through seeing more patients", and "a competitive advantage" for respondents' hospitals40. So, AI might be good for business, which seems to be what these respondents tended to prioritize. *But what about patient care?*

Remember the panel discussion at the veterinary conference, where it was emphasized that "ICU" should mean *I see you;* where veterinarians were urged to observe the entire patient and not only their vital signs? AI may be able to do many things (and veterinary hospitals are reportedly already using it to assist with everything from imaging and radiology to triage, diagnosis, and disease detection, as well as record keeping, administrative tasks, and the ever-more-important *marketing*) but it is not able- at least not yet- to make a subjective assessment of pain, fear, or stress in a veterinary patient based on the patient's behavior, facial expressions, and attitude. It's not able (and will *never* be able) to provide a reassuring, soothing, *human* presence to an animal experiencing distress- or to that animal's human caregiver either, for that matter.

In addition to survey-reported concerns about the current reliability and accuracy (or lack thereof) of AI systems, *my* concern is that AI in veterinary medicine will amount to a tiny Band-Aid slapped over a sucking chest wound of problems while being hailed as a cure-all, and that it will be over-relied upon to the detriment of patients. I fear it will become the newest *excuse* for management refusing to hire enough human personnel; the latest *reason why* practice owners *still* believe a skeleton crew will be sufficient, and that in effect it will help to *perpetuate* the veterinary industry's staffing woes, rather than effectively helping teams work better together. I fear it will become the reason the corporate number-crunchers will believe they can (and should!) crunch even *more*. And how many errors in diagnosis, disease detection, triage, or drug dose calculation will occur and be accepted as inevitable while the accuracy and reliability of these systems gradually improves? Do you want *your* pet to be one of the test cases?

The use of AI in general may also eventually bring some thorny ethical questions, and I've actually not even scratched the surface of the snarl of already-existing ethical questions that touch on the veterinary world- issues such as the industry-endorsed treatment of livestock animals in the meat, dairy, and egg industries, among others- since my experience has only been in companion animal practices.

Companion animals- and the branch of veterinary medicine focusing on them- occupy a unique and strange place in our society. As veterinary professionals, we're supposed to treat our patients essentially as if they're human... but we don't, not really. We *can't*, not fully. So there are all these gray areas- morally and ethically speaking- and all these things that hospitals can get away with that wouldn't be permitted in human medicine. And the patients have no choice about any of it, and don't even fully understand what's happening to them.

The movement to change the legal status of companion animals has been gaining momentum in recent years, as societal norms and attitudes regarding petkeeping have been changing and science has revealed more about animals' cognitive abilities and social development. If we agree that the law is a reflection of the norms and values in a society, then we must also agree that companion animals' legal status as property is inconsistent with their current *cultural* status as members of our families, and this inconsistency often negatively impacts not only animals, but their human guardians as well[41].

Clearly, the lack of regulation and oversight in the veterinary industry is a prime example of this, and many legal experts believe that animals must be removed from the category of property in order to be granted meaningful legal protections. To create a new legal status for pets designating them as "nonhuman legal persons" (as has been done for ships and corporations in the U.S. and for individual nonhuman animals as well as lakes and rivers in countries outside the U.S.[42]) would not be so great a leap from already-existing animal-cruelty laws-extant in all 50 states- which treat cats and dogs fundamentally differently from other types of property. But the veterinary world has historically opposed efforts to elevate or enhance the legal status of companion animals, primarily due to fears of increased malpractice awards[43], just as it has thus far opposed legislation seeking to ban declawing due to fears of lost clients and lost revenue.

I have heard veterinarians telling clients that if veterinary patients were ever to be granted meaningful protection under the law, then veterinary care would immediately be priced out of most clients' reach due to the massive increase in malpractice insurance every DVM would then be forced to carry. But this is happening to many caregivers already for other reasons which do *not* benefit or protect us or our animals; we are gradually being conditioned to accept that pet insurance is becoming a necessity to afford to keep a companion animal at all, but the standard of care is not rising along with costs. It seems to me that one obvious solution to this conundrum would be for DVMs to do their utmost to ensure that they are not committing malpractice in the *first* place, so they are not viewed by insurers as a high risk. Changing the legal status of their patients might be just what's needed to motivate the industry to do this across the board.

I can hear the indignation of the profession now in response to this book: "Stop discouraging people from seeking veterinary care for their animals!" Let me be very clear: that is not my intention. I do NOT wish to discourage anyone from seeking veterinary care; it's my firm belief that the provision of healthcare is a fundamental part of being a responsible and loving pet parent. It isn't *optional.* Therefore, rather than discouraging anyone, I want to *en*courage caregivers to seek the *best* veterinary care they can find and access. They must understand, of course, that quality healthcare in the United States does come at a significant cost, and there is no longer much difference between the human medical sphere and the veterinary world in this regard, unfortunately. For decades, veterinary care has perhaps *seemed* more affordable than it truly should have been, because hospitals have been under so little scrutiny and have been permitted to operate in any way they see fit. Caregivers must also understand that improving these conditions and raising standards may further affect the fees they can expect to pay, since the increasing corporatization of vet med does not come with a guarantee of any particular standard of care. I want pet parents to be better informed about issues within the profession which can impact their pet's quality of care so that they may have a better chance of avoiding some of them. I want to empower them to ask questions at their vet clinic, to express their concerns, and to trust their intuition when something doesn't feel right to them. Doctors or staff who view this as being "demanding" are being unreasonable themselves, in my opinion, and should perhaps reexamine their reasons for entering a field where their entire job is supposed to be to support the human-animal bond.

"Stop fostering hatred against vets! Don't you know the veterinary profession has the highest rate of suicide?" Yes- I'm well aware of this, and nor is "fostering hatred" my intention here. There are *good* vets in my story as well as distressing ones, and there are those who *try* to be good, but who are imperfect, flawed human beings, as we all ultimately are. The veterinary world has been *my* world; the veterinary community has been *my* community, and as I stated at the beginning, my criticism of it comes out of love, not hatred. Individual veterinarians may have (rightfully) earned my anger, but the fact that veterinary professionals die by suicide at a greater rate than members of other professions is not something to which I am insensitive.

This is not a new or recent phenomenon, either; as far back as my first job in the late 90s, my co-workers and I were talking about the tragically high rate of suicide among veterinarians, and veterinary professionals in supporting roles. But in the 90s we didn't blame our "demanding, ungrateful" clients (and the veterinary world has always had its share, just like any other industry which serves the public) or the everyday stresses of the job- even those unique to our profession. Rather, we talked about the fact that people who choose to work in veterinary medicine often do so because to some degree (and sometimes a *large* degree), we are not "people persons". This can make it harder to feel that you fit well into society, and it can limit your social ties in comparison to other people.

This is a fundamental difference between veterinary professionals and their colleagues in human medicine, where a similar access to certain kinds of drugs also enables a high rate of substance abuse and mental health issues among personnel. But only veterinary medicine also has drugs specifically designed for euthanasia, and this is another fundamental difference; the acceptance of euthanasia in the veterinary profession can make "self-euthanasia" seem a more attractive option when life becomes hard.

I do get it, you see?

Interestingly, however, I only started noticing the suicide statistic being talked about more openly as the veterinary world began to fall under more public scrutiny and criticism, due (at least in part) to its interference in the progress of the movement to end declawing. Not One More Vet, a nonprofit organization dedicated to raising awareness of the status of mental health within the profession (and whose name is a direct reference to the suicide rate), was founded in 2014- coincidentally, the year after the release of the Paw Project's self-titled documentary detailing the extent to which veterinary industry lobbyists in California fought *hard* to keep declawing legal there. Many viewers of the film wondered why the veterinary community would be so vehemently *against* legislation to protect its patients, and for a brief time, the hashtag #NotOneMoreCat was circulating concurrently on Twitter (now "X") in reference to the number of cats still being declawed in the United States.

Suddenly, virtually every social media disagreement between veterinary professionals and laypersons- regardless of topic and however minor- began seeming to prompt citations of the suicide statistic and accusations of "cyberbullying" from the former, and once the "mass exodus" of 2020 began amidst the pandemic, battle lines were drawn ever more starkly between "us"- the world of vet med- and "them"- the outside world which can't (or won't) understand all the hardships veterinary professionals face. While I do not wish to imply that this has been in any way deliberate or intentional on the part of Not One More Vet (which is also doing vital work to help provide mental health education, resources, and support to veterinary professionals in crisis), I'm not the only "pro-claw" activist who has noticed or commented on this correlation. And while nobody wants to see veterinary professionals ending their own lives, *nor* should they be using this tragic statistic as a kind of shield against valid criticism of the industry as a whole, or against clients who may have legitimate complaints. I'm disturbed by the apparent willingness I'm seeing within the profession to grossly oversimplify a complex issue- and attempt to silence those who question or find fault with any aspect of vet med- by claiming that "people are losing their lives *all because of people like YOU*" (a verbatim quote hurled at me on social media).

There's simply more to it than that. Veterinary work is *hard*, in many different ways. It's very hard for caring people to work with animals- and *for* animals- on someone else's terms, and to depend financially on their ability to do so. It's very hard to protect one's heart under those circumstances. If my veterinary career taught me nothing else, it certainly taught me *that*. Practice owners and management should be sensitive to the mental health needs of their staff members and make a concerted effort to reduce or eliminate sources of moral or financial distress they may be facing. This might require allowing them to decline to participate in things like declawing or convenience euthanasia of healthy animals if they have a moral objection to doing so, or it might require supporting the growing efforts of veterinary schools and state governments to further subsidize the cost of a veterinary medical degree. (In the case of hospitals owned by corporate franchises seeing annual profits in billions of dollars, the CEOs might consider creating more scholarships and grant opportunities for vet students, as well, to help alleviate some of the crushing debt under which so many new graduates later find themselves laboring.) Team leaders must also respect and protect their employees' work/life balance (which requires investing in your staff, hiring enough qualified personnel, and making sure they feel valued enough to stay), rather than trying to deflect blame onto concerned pet caregivers or animal welfare activists for their workers' suffering.

While writing this memoir, I strained to recall any specific encounter with a "demanding, ungrateful" client that stood out in my mind as causing me distress, and I honestly could not- despite the fact that receptionists usually end up interacting with clients more frequently and longer than DVMs do, and take the brunt of clients' complaints when they're unhappy. (Even Grendel's caregivers at Dr. Z.'s hospital were memorable only for their lack of empathy for Grendel herself.) I remember *numerous* specific examples of feeling unsupported, devalued, bullied, or exploited by my employers, however. A strong and effective veterinary team requires *good* leadership above all, and I mean "good" in every sense of the word. While writing this book, I finally began to grasp the extent to which inept and/or corrupt leadership and management have been at the sickened heart of American veterinary medicine for as long as I've known it, and likely longer.

This is an understanding that is beautifully elucidated by Anthony Pierlioni in his 2023 book *Veterinary Leadership Through Fresh Eyes: A Social Worker's Approach To Veterinary Management.* In it, he exhorts readers to "Remember the main focus of a veterinary leader. Our most pivotal role is to support our teams who work tirelessly to care for our patients. They leave their blood, sweat, and tears on the treatment room floor. The least we can do is give them our attention. Any adult just wants to feel like their opinions, sacrifices, and efforts are noticed and appreciated. The first way to lose them is missing this opportunity."[44] And when it comes to dealing with clients, Pierlioni acknowledges: "Make no mistake about it, we are busy. Busier than ever, in fact. We cannot, however, allow this fact to affect the way we treat those around us... we are judged based on how we make (clients) feel."[45] He stresses the importance of understanding the *human* working relationships that make up a veterinary team, and pinpoints some of the worst and most common problems teams face. I found myself nodding emphatically and underlining passages as I read this book, and I hope it will find its way to some of the people who need to read it the most.

Those preparing for careers as veterinary professionals today- and those choosing to remain after the "mass exodus"- would probably do well to accept that their profession, while equally demanding and difficult as human medicine (if not *more* so), will never be equally valued by society, because their patients are not human. This is the reason for the substantially lower salaries that veterinarians and veterinary professionals can expect to earn compared to their counterparts in human medicine, and the reason why the *best* veterinary professionals have never entered the field because it's a high-paying or high-prestige career, but because it's a labor of love. It's best viewed as a *calling*, not a career; a *passion* rather than a paycheck. Unfortunately, not everyone with the right level of passion for helping animals can afford to indulge it- especially if hospitals think they can simply implement an AI system to do the job at a lower cost to them.

This is perhaps one area in which the National Veterinary Professionals Union may be able to help. Established in 2017 in California, the NVPU's goals include empowering veterinary support staff to band together and collectively bargain for change in their workplaces, establishing realistic staff-to-patient ratios to ensure the safety of both, advocating for patients and the provision of gold-standard care, and negotiating for and enforcing payment of a living wage for veterinary support staff46. The union is still in its early stages according to its website, and in need of support, but its existence makes me feel much more optimistic than the thought of AI diagnosing my children's medical conditions and formulating their treatment plans. I wish this organization had existed years and years ago, and I sincerely hope they will get the support they need to become a force for positive change within the industry.

In the following quote from NVPU's "Frequently Asked Questions", I can read between the lines and see that a *lot* of veterinary support staff are tired of dealing with all the same kinds of issues I've been describing here from my own experiences:

"If all veterinary facilities do not accept a burden of ethical responsibility for their employees, then their patients will suffer the consequences of poor patient care due to inadequate veterinary professional to patient ratios, poor and ineffective staff recruitment and retention, employee bullying, workplace health and safety issues, etc. By creating a union, we hope to bring the industry into alignment and level the playing field by making sure everyone is playing the same game."[47]

Labor unions can be a touchy subject for many people, and pet caregivers may understandably be concerned about what strikes could potentially mean for patient care in hospitals where the staff have organized, but NVPU has already addressed the need for careful planning to avoid disruptions to patient care, including adequate notice and working with management, and observes that in reality, fewer than 2% of union contract negotiations across the country lead to strikes[48]. One of NVPU's main long-term goals is *accountability* at all levels of veterinary practice, and I hope that my story will illustrate to pet parents just how badly this is needed, and will encourage them to support the NVPU's efforts.

What I hope it will *not* do is cause anyone to completely write off the profession or decide that their pet doesn't really need to see the vet. Yes, there are longstanding problems the veterinary world urgently needs to address. And yes, capitalism and corporatization are pushing veterinary care in a disturbing direction which exacerbates these problems (pandemic or no pandemic). But we caregivers can't just throw up our hands and throw out the baby with the bathwater; our animals deserve better than that. We must be informed, aware, and responsible. We must all be our animals' advocates.

Difficulty in *accessing* veterinary care is likely to persist for years to come, and may get worse before it gets better; Mars Veterinary Health estimates there will be a deficit of veterinarians in the U.S. to the tune of 15,000 by 2030[49]. Pet parents as distressed as I am by the situation should arm themselves with as much information about their animal's health conditions as they can, and learn how to provide emergency first aid and CPR for them at home if the need arises.

Don't choose a hospital or a doctor based on their reviews alone; like reviews for any other service, these can be faked by practice owners or managers (yes, I witnessed this once as well), and even legitimate reviews posted by real clients of the hospital may not always be truly meaningful. Most will focus on the customer service experience alone, because it can be difficult for many clients to accurately assess the quality of medical care received by their pet. Do *read* a hospital's reviews, but take them with a grain of salt, and trust your own experience and observations more. Get second opinions, third opinions, as many opinions as you need to feel you're making the best possible decisions for your pets.

Be observant when you visit your veterinary clinic; don't spend your entire wait time staring at your phone. Notice if the exam room looks clean and organized (or if it doesn't). Observe the way the staff members seem to be feeling, and the way they interact with each other as well as with you and your pet. Do they seem like they make a good team, like they work together well? Do they seem happy to be there? It can make a difference in the care your pet receives. Hospitals which value their team members highly will also place a higher value on the work that they do, and will usually have a happier team as a result. Obviously, no human being (and no healthcare team made up of human beings) is capable of having a great day *every* day- but try to notice if there are obvious patterns from one appointment to the next. Remember that however fallible human beings can be, an automated system can malfunction, too, but the automated system can't *care* that it did. Speak up to the DVM or the practice manager about staff members who shine in your opinion; express your appreciation. Let management know that you- as the paying client- want to see the support team supported in turn. Let them know you care about their credentials, as well. Let them know if you have reservations or concerns about the use of AI in the hospital.

And if your pet's clinic is chronically understaffed and you're in need of additional income, it can't hurt to ask them if they could use help. I realize I probably haven't made veterinary support work sound very attractive, but despite everything I've related here, it's still- like the Peace Corps says- "the toughest job I ever loved". Not everyone should leap straight into working as a vet tech or nurse (even if that's legal in your state!), but anyone can use a broom or a mop; anyone can clean cages, anyone can take some of the workload off the plates of those with more specialized training... if only the practice owners and managers will hire them.

Good help *is* still out there, and it need not be artificial intelligence. Team leaders should search for the people who *understand* the work that needs to be done, and who have true passion for doing it. Some might even be willing to *volunteer* their time, if you'll only let them.

In recent decades, veterinary hospitals have shied away from allowing volunteers to step in and help because they fall into a murky legal category in regard to professional liability and labor laws. But if human medicine can still utilize the work of trained volunteers (and it does), then it would seem there should be a way for the veterinary world to figure out how to implement its own "candy striper" programs, and I believe these could be extremely valuable- not only for patient care right now, but also for future generations of veterinary professionals, so that they can embark on their careers with their eyes fully open in regard to the hard realities of working in this field (something the current generation, burning out and leaving at such an alarming rate, could probably have benefited from).

This might require the industry to petition the federal government to allow an exception to the Fair Labor Standards Act which prohibits the use of volunteer labor in for-profit organizations, citing the veterinary profession's current overwhelming need for staff. Or it might require written agreements between volunteers and employers specifically detailing the scope of tasks and duties the volunteers may undertake and what they may not. I'm no legal expert, but again: if it can be figured out for human medicine (despite many hospitals being for-profit just as veterinary hospitals are), then I fail to see why it cannot be figured out for veterinary medicine, which is equally important to public health. And right now, vet med needs anyone who wants to help.

Anyone can be an extra pair of gentle hands to give a comforting caress, and an extra pair of caring eyes looking out for the patients who are falling through the cracks- the *truest* consumers of veterinary services, whose very lives depend upon us getting it right.

EPILOGUE

In March of 2024, just as I was nearing the end of this writing, a report was published by the American Animal Hospital Association entitled *Stay, Please: A Challenge To The Veterinary Profession To Improve Employee Retention.* Based on the results of an online survey conducted the previous year with over 14,000 respondents, the report "reaffirmed the disquieting fact that a tremendous number of the profession's workforce is planning to leave their current position."[50] Asked about their reasons for wanting to leave versus what could persuade them to stay, respondents overwhelmingly indicated that fair compensation, feeling valued at work, opportunities for career development, and good teamwork are the biggest things they need and are *not* getting.[51] This sounds very, very familiar to me.

While on one hand I suppose it's good that the industry is finally beginning to *acknowledge* that it suffers from a staffing crisis (and that the endless supply of "starry eyed young people" is not seeming so endless anymore), the primary feeling I had upon reading AAHA's report was that the insights it reveals are extremely basic- elementary, in fact- and that such a survey and such a report should not really have been necessary.

It should never have been any kind of mystery to hospital owners or managers that paying employees well and treating them fairly are the main things that make them want to stay in their positions; this is after all true in *any* industry. And the report also overcomplicates the issue (in my opinion) by spending significant time discussing a "role-based approach" to appeal to three categories of "veterinary profession personas"[52], suggesting that different kinds of people need different kinds of rewards from the work that they do. Maybe so, but *every* employee needs to be compensated and treated as if they *matter* to the business, and that is exactly how veterinary support staff have-overwhelmingly- *not* been treated by the industry as a whole, for far too long.

I also find it a bit worrisome that the report can identify something like "flexibility of work scheduling" as an extremely valuable factor in employee retention, yet completely neglect to mention that the only real way to offer such flexibility is to have *more workers to cover shifts.* Without this, "flexibility" becomes a vaguely defined and ultimately unattainable thing. A skeleton crew can never be flexible with its employee work schedules. I worry that the report is long on information that should have already been well understood or intuited, and short on specific, *simple,* and concrete ways to fix what's wrong. It's looking at the problem too abstractly for my liking.

Still, the fact that the industry is finally beginning to address these issues in *any* way represents a step in the right direction, and AAHA's stated goals (to "form the foundation for a new veterinary employment paradigm" and "bring joy back to the professionals who were made for this and deliver the support and resources that remind them they were built to last"53) are admirable ones.

For the sake of the animals we share our world and our lives with, let's hope they can figure out how to accomplish these goals *fast.*

-END-

REFERENCES

1. DVM360 magazine, July 2023, Vol. 54, Issue 7
2. The Atlantic, July 6, 2022 (theatlantic.com/health/archive/ 2022/07/not-enough-veterinarians-animals)
3. Encyclopedia Britannica online (britannica.com/science/ veterinary-medicine)
4. World History Encyclopedia online (worldhistory.org/ article/1549/a-brief-history-of-veterinary-medicine)
5. Ibid.
6. Ibid.
7. Farm Journal Foundation report, December 6, 2022 (farmjournalfoundation.org/post/rural-veterinary-shortages-create-risks-for-food-system-report-says)
8. "Can I Sue My Vet For Malpractice?", NOLO (nolo.com/ legal-encyclopedia/free-books/dog-book/chapter5-8.html)
9. National Association Of Veterinary Technicians In America, February 2022. (navta.net/news/navta-report-shows-title-protection-for-veterinary-technician-is-needed-and-desired-but-absent-and-misunderstood-in-most-states/)
10. Encyclopedia.com/science/ encyclopedias-almanacs-transcripts-and-maps/veterinarians-oath #:~:text=Originally%20adopted%20by%20the%20AVMA,were%2(
11. American Veterinary Medical Association (avma.org/ resources-tools/avma-policies/veterinarians-oath)
12. "New Veterinary Startup Emerges From Stealth Mode", DVM360 magazine, July 2023
13. DVM360 magazine, July 2023, Vol. 54, Issue 7
14. The Paw Project Frequently Asked Questions (https://pawproject.org/about-declawing/faqs/)
15. The Theory Of Mammalian Life, copyright 2018 by Jordyn

Hewer, DVM

16. DVM360 magazine, 7-24-23, Vol. 54, Issue 7 "Celebrating Our Veterinary Heroes"

17. World Wide Words (https://www.worldwidewords.org/qa/qa-red2.htm#:~:text=A%20true%20stepchild%20in%20a,headed%2...

18. Pictures Of Cats (https://pictures-of-cats.org/origin-of-cat-declawing.html)

19. Journal of the American Veterinary Medical Association (JAVMA), November 1952

20. Ibid.

21. American Association of Feline Practitioners (https://catvets.com/claw-friendly-toolkit/scientific-literature)

22. The Providence Journal, June 12, 2023 (https://www.providencejournal.com/story/news/politics/2023/06/12/cat-declawing-ban-bill-passes-ri-senate-heads-to-house-rivma-opposed/70303612007/)

23. UC Davis Young Scholars Program, "Measuring and Predicting Syringe Hub Loss" (https://ysprogram.ucdavis.edu/content/measuring-and-predicting-syringe-hub-loss)

24. American Animal Hospital Association (AAHA), "Update On Feline Injection-Site Sarcomas" (https://www.aaha.org/aaha-guidelines/2020-aahaaafp-feline-vaccination-guidelines/update-injection-site-sarcoma/)

25. "The Corporatization Of Veterinary Medicine", copyright November 2018, JAVMA News (https://www.avma.org/javma-news/2018-12-01/corporatization-veterinary-medicine#:~:text=Depending%20on%20the%20source%2C%20the,abou...

26. "Why A Cat Hospital?" copyright 2023, Cats Exclusive Veterinary Center website (https://www.catsexclusive.com/why-a-cat-hospital#:~:text=Cats%20Exclusive%20Veterinary%20Hospital%2

27. Norsworthy, Gary D., DVM, DABVP, ed. The Feline Patient. John Wiley & Sons, 2018. 977-984.

28. "Why Feline-Only Veterinary Clinics Are Worth It", copyright January 2023, Petful.com. (https://www.petful.com/behaviors/feline-only-veterinary-clinics/)

29. "Toxoplasmosis: An Important Message For Cat Owners", The Centers For Disease Control (https://www.cdc.gov/parasites/toxoplasmosis/toxoplasmosis_catowners.html#:~:text=It%20is%20unlikely%20that%20you,

30. "Kittengarden Lets Cats, Owners Bond", Associated Press via The Denver Post, January 2009 (updated May 2016) (https://www.denverpost.com/2009/01/08/kittengarden-lets-cats-owners-bond/)

31. "Comparison of 3 Methods of Onychectomy" , The Canadian Veterinary Journal, March 2014 (https://www.ncbi.nlm.nih.gov/pmc/articles/PMC3923482/)

32. "Our History", Louisiana SPCA (https://www.louisianaspca.org/about-us/our-history/#/)

33. "The Bridge To Gretna", CBS News, December 2005 (https://www.cbsnews.com/news/the-bridge-to-gretna/)

34. "Vet techs: A fulfilling career may be waiting outside the clinic", DVM360, December 2021 (https://www.dvm360.com/view/vet-techs-a-fulfilling-career-may-be-waiting-outside-the-clinic)

35. "Elderly Cats-Special Considerations", copyright July 2018, International Cat Care (https://icatcare.org/advice/elderly-cats-special-considerations/#:~:text=In%20recent%20years%2C%20feline%20ages,their%

36. "The Dark Side Of Constant Optimism", Psychology Today, October 2022 (https://www.psychologytoday.com/us/blog/you-are-not-meant-be-happy/202210/the-dark-side-constant-optimism)

37. "The Barrier Of 'The Back'", DVM360, July 2023 (https://www.dvm360.com/view/the-barrier-of-the-back-)

38. "Creating Brighter Futures For Cats With Chronic Kidney Disease", JAVMA News, January 2021 (https://www.avma.org/javma-news/2021-02-01/creating-brighter-futures-cats-chronic-kidney-disease)

39. "AI In Veterinary Medicine: The Next Paradigm Shift", pdf copyright 2024 by Digitail (https://4912130.fs1.hubspotusercontent-na1.net/hubfs/4912130/Whitepapers/Digitail%20AI%20in%20Veterinary%20Medicine%20Study.pdf?utm_me

40. Ibid.

41. "Chattel or Child: The Liminal Status of Companion Animals In Society & Law", copyright 2019, Nicole R. Pallotta, The Animal Legal Defense Fund

42. Ibid.

43. "Not A Living Room Sofa: Changing The Legal Status of Companion Animals", copyright 2007, Susan J. Hankin, University of Maryland School of Law

44. Veterinary Leadership Through Fresh Eyes: A Social Worker's Approach To Veterinary Management, copyright 2023 by Anthony Pierlioni

45. Ibid.

46. National Veterinary Professionals Union website (https://www.natvpu.org)

47. Ibid.

48. Ibid.

49. "Unraveling the Veterinary Industry Staff Shortage: How did we get here?" copyright August 2023 by ezyVet

(https://www.ezyvet.com/blog/unraveling-the-veterinary-industry-staff-shortage-how-did-we-get-here)

50. "Stay, Please: A Challenge To The Veterinary Profession To Improve Employee Retention" copyright March 2024, American Animal Hospital Association (https://www.aaha.org/practice-resources/research-center/white-paper-form-the-path-to-increasing-retention-in-veterinary-medicine/)

51. Ibid.

52. Ibid.

53. Ibid.